VINAIGRETTE

~because life is bitter and sweet~

Linda C. Barrett

ISBN-10: 1727489322

ISBN-13: 978-1727489323

Cover Photo Credit: Tamara Kulikova

DEDICATION

This work is dedicated to the Holy Trinity: This is a work of obedience, and a tribute to YOU and the work you've done in my heart. Thank you for leading me and giving me the privilege of declaring your praise. I am especially grateful for your grace, for without it, I would not have survived the shame of my sin, imperfection, and failure.

Also, to my beloved friends and family, who have journeyed with me through the oil and vinegar of life. I would not know what I know or be who I am without your corporate love, patience, and wisdom. You have poured oil on my wounds and pointed me to Christ when I suffered. I am also thankful for your willingness to share your sorrows with me. Your transparency has helped me be more honest with myself.

FOREWORD

Vinaigrette

Sorrow and Joy –
    an odd chemistry whose elements do not form solution
    like oil and vinegar – one soothing – one acerbic.
I shake them together
    desperately
    hoping that they might fuse into one sweet union.
Fuse!
They refuse.
Without debate it's poured like vinaigrette on my life.
Compelled to consume
The bitter-sweet potion. I must choose.
                        Die; or eat and live.

We live in a bittersweet world. We long for the sweet. We do whatever we can to obtain it and grasp and cling to it when it comes near. However, sorrow, sin, fear, and doubt are also features of our lives. To deny their existence is self-deceptive, and won't produce a cure. Brennan Manning says, in *The Rabbi's Heartbeat*, "What is denied cannot be healed."

When Paul complained of his thorn in the flesh, Christ answered the protest with, *"My grace is enough for you. When you are weak, my power is made perfect in you."* Paul's response? *"So I am very happy to brag about my weaknesses. Then Christ's power can live in me."* (II Cor. 12:9 NCV)

It's sobering to admit weakness; however, our humble and brutal honesty about our need is the key to receiving the full abundant grace of God. As we admit our prodigal living and personal weaknesses, our Father runs to us and brings forgiveness for our sin, comfort for sorrow, and his abundant love and absolute acceptance for self-hatred.

The first time I remember experiencing paradoxical emotions simultaneously was thirty-five years ago during worship when my husband was unemployed. We had two small children. I was afraid and depressed. Unable to see beyond the present heartache, I felt shame and a sense of mounting failure and despair. Wrenched with dark emotions, I worshiped in obedience that day. I lifted my hands and face and began to thank and praise God with what my heart could offer. Tears of sorrow and joy poured down my face as I offered a sacrifice of praise. I extolled the God who was faithful (though he didn't seem to be), and the God who loves and never forsakes his own. I didn't like where God had me, but still, in the middle of that dark place, I felt the joy of obedience and the presence of God as I worshiped. It was the first of many similar moments, and one I'll never forget.

This collection of poems, reflections, and perspectives presents this bitter/sweet reality in which we live—our vinaigrette. My prayer is that the honesty of *my* conflicting emotions in these poems will help you fully embrace the oil and vinegar of your own dazzlingly mysterious life.

WHY VINAIGRETTE WAS WRITTEN

In the winter of 2017, my oldest son brought me some books of poetry written by a patient he was treating. (Per her request) She passed away later. As I read them, I realized I met the author at a poetry reading about five to ten years earlier. I tried meeting with her after we met, but our paths never crossed again—until my son brought me those books.

After reading them, I regretted that I gave up trying to get to know her. Regret. That is one reason I began this project. I don't want the regret of cowardice, and I would regret NOT publishing my poems. Her bravery to self-publish un-extraordinary writing encouraged me.

Many friends have also asked me to put my work into an available collection. The sudden mortal illness of a friend pushed me, as well. Death can arrive unexpectedly for any of us. I hate the thought of all my poetry being lost in a desolate Apple computer graveyard—unread, unremembered, or unable to be recalled.

When I told friends about my plans to compile and publish, I received three offers of financial support to help in the process. This was a confirming voice for me. I began the lengthy process in January of 2018.

******

I was first introduced to poetry in the fifth grade and hated most of it. In high school, I re-discovered it when I went on a Baptist youth retreat—of all places. The speaker used poems to emphasize certain points. (I recently found the Parker Memorial retreat brochure amongst old high school memorabilia. Phew, I didn't dream it.) After that retreat, poetry became a new friend. That began my use of poetry to reflect about life and to process the many conflicting emotions I experience.

When God formed me, he put an artist inside. That artist paints, does crafts, writes, and even makes music. I've always responded to the world more seriously than most. I was a quiet, pensive child, and due to necessity, spent much time alone. It made me deeply aware of the world, others, and myself.

God also made me curious about himself. I've enjoyed that part of my life best. I love discovering God in Scripture, worshipping him in community, and growing in my faith through prayer, meditation, and the teachings of others.

Early on, I realized that when God showed me something about himself, I couldn't keep quiet about it. When I found a treasure, I felt compelled to share it. In that attempt, I've been obnoxious and abrasive when I should have been compassionate, judgmental when I should have listened and offered grace, and prideful instead of humble. I've also been a shame-filled wreck when I couldn't live the truths I knew in my head and heart—and before I began to understand the depth of God's grace.

A friend of mine once said **of me**, "I see because you show me." It was an important message for me. And that's what I want to do. I want to show you what I've seen of God through my sin, doubt, self-contempt, madness, and fear.

I want to offer comfort in your sorrow and rest in your wrestling. I want to give you permission to laugh at yourself when you are too serious. I want you to receive God's forgiveness when you live sinfully, and I want to pour out grace by the bucket load. I hope that you will feel the freedom to admit your debilitating fears and tormenting anger and know that there is a God waiting offstage. He waits for you to take off the mask and come to him with everything—EVERYTHING you are and all the contradictory emotions you feel.

HOW TO CONSUME VINAIGRETTE

I begin each chapter with a prayer about the topics. The poems follow. At the end of each section of poetry, there are "Personal Reflections" that contain three or four Scripture verses and questions upon which you can mediate as you chew on the ideas in the chapter. In "Poet's Perspective" at the back of the book, I write an explanation as to why each poem was written. The curious can find answers there.

In addition to being a book of poetry, *Vinaigrette* can be a twelve-week devotional. It could also be used in a small-group discussion with an emphasis on God's Word in the "Personal Reflections." A teacher could add other Scripture for enrichment.

May God's Spirit penetrate your heart with the hope that is here and bring sweetness into the bitterness of your life.

Table of Contents

Poet's Perspective

Chapter I
SELF-LOATHING AND
THE LOVE OF GOD

Father, so much of my life has been filled with self-loathing. Growing to accept my life as a gift remains challenging, but one you've helped me face and believe. I suppose the healing began when I first understood the depth of your love and your grace. It was as I saw you loving me—in all my sin and shame, in all my failures and brokenness, in all my anger and self-hatred, that I began to know that I was worthy of your love—not because I *was* worthy, but because you declared it so.

You called me your own. Your beloved. Your precious child. Who can hate oneself when one is loved so audaciously? So madly? So unrelentingly and unrepentantly by one so gloriously good? My coldness did not chill your love. My ambivalence did not cool your passion. My self-despising only brought more compassion and sympathy—sympathy that I didn't understand you, didn't comprehend you—or me. Sometimes I have hated how you made me. Skinny. Fat. Weak. Sinful. With allergies and bad eyesight, prone to depression and unhealthy emotions. Contaminated by old evils done to me and done by me. Shame. Fear—always fear.

But you've allowed me to see your smiling face and your delight in me. And O, how I love you for it! Your love stirs me. It woos me to face my fears. To accept my weakness and embrace your power in me. It sings over me and encourages me to worship the God who made me—just like you made the mountains and the hills, and the oceans and skies. You've taken me on a journey to the center of your love: a discovery of grace and the power of the cross, and I'm so thankful. I've encountered you over and over again. Your love erodes the negative thoughts that torment me. Because of it, I can pen this prayer. I can expose my life—unashamed— because the God who made heaven and earth is my Father, and he loves me. And your love has transformed me—grace by grace, kiss by kiss, forgiveness by forgiveness, delight by delight.

So Lord, I dedicate this section of poems to your unrelenting love.

GOMER   (from the book of Hosea)

You wait for me to let you fold my heart
Into your love and lose myself in eyes
So deep with love my breath breaks and sighs.
But I resist and will not yield to you.

You chose me, wed me, bed me, sired babes
Then insulted me with their names. What were
You about as you drew me with eyes but
Scorched me with words so blistering, I ran?

Of course I had been unfaithful, but you
Knew what I was when you chose me
On the streets – a wounded, wicked, and willful woman.
I ran to strangers' arms swiftly and was snared.

You chased me down in wild wonder, buying
Me for two cents on the dollar, cheapened
By a thousand lovers and then beaten
By those very hands that had caressed me.

Now, once again, I am yours as slave –
Yet you do not want me as this.

You smile – engaging, inviting, wooing. I turn hard –
Your smiles and kindness anger me.

I mock your tenderness and care and choose to dread faithful love.
I waken to chores, children and chaste love.
I am hardened, but you are a fool,
Pursuing me with eyes and gentleness.

You laugh at some small joke – engaging me.
I turn my head and roll my eyes,
But I smile inside – feeling safe with your longing sigh.
I glance at your face and see the sorrow drawn.

Can it be? Only a fool would love me.
Would want me. Devious, cunning woman
That I am. Soiled and unaccustomed to kind
And tender words or undemanding touch.

I cannot bear the kindness. It wears and wounds me.
You must be a fool. Only a fool would love me.
I waken in the night – you look at me with the longing
Of a thousand lovers – I look back and touch your face.

Tenderly, without demands, you hold me.
Day after day, we replay the dance.
But today, I smile back and laugh.
I see you work and speak and act.

It is good. You are no fool.
Except that you choose to love me.

Today – perhaps today, I will allow you to fold me
Into love and I will lose myself in your eyes.

CREATOR'S PRAISE

A snow-capped peak oft' leads my soul to praise.
A babbling brook, toads croaking in the night,
And suns that set o'er seas in scarlet glaze,
All lead my soul to worship in delight.

I bow in awe before tempestuous seas.
In blissful joy I sing when blooms unwind,
And yield their lively fragrance, luring bees.
And I breathe in the glory - still my mind.

And then I hear a voice that beckons, "Come.
Look in the mirror. Tell me what is there.
Please see the wonder lovely, though undone.
And worship me with loving thankful prayer."

With tears I praise him then with outstretched hands,
For what I'm yet to be and who I am.

MY PARADIGM - MY WORDS

These words emerge from my paradigm.

Yours will not do.

My words leached through this skin
My thoughts dripping from my brow
Like sweat in labor
        Perspiration in heat
And sometimes it stinks – just so.

Yet, it can glisten in the sunshine
or form tracks across my face,
creating gleaming evidence of painful toil
and cooling my body like fine sweat should.

THE F WORD

I hate the "F" word.
It speaks of evil.
Its vile sound still echoes in my 6-year-old ears.
The word is unredeemable,
Unlike the act it supposedly describes.
It publicizes glory being shattered,
Innocence stolen,
Violence done.
I HATE the "F" word.

CRY ALOUD

Cry aloud and seek a face that does not give back mocking,
But hears and guides and answers as a faithful father should.
Leading us along with words so fit and right
Our heart aches with the discovery, and mourns our loss –
Years of deafness when we did not hear.

And so we press on with tears and pleadings and with
Outstretched arms – longing for the more of His supply.
And never are we met with stones or asps or evil's dark answer,
But mercy awaits us – and holiness and wisdom, and glory that exceeds our prayers
And sheds light on our pleadings
That are answered out of a character so fine…

Our breath is taken from us.

SACRED ROMANCE

Creator speaks his words, across the darkened void.
Light springs up awakened, Creator laughs with joy.

The seas alive now churn; God-driven words have made.
Each finny creature seen there, made free and unafraid.

Pulsing from the ground, the trees and plants spring forth
From all points on the globe - east, west, and south and north.

The sun is set in motion; in space, the planets whirl.
The stars move forth in triumph; the firmaments unfurl.

From nothing springs each creature, awakened by God's Word.
Each deer and bug and lizard, each snake and fish and bird.

The earth erupts in praises, to God's majestic strength,
And God smiles at the sound of it, and then, pauses and thinks.

Then stepping through the shimmer, he grabs a lump of earth,
And molding it with gentle hands, he breathes man into birth.

Then man stands fully wakened, and woman joins him there,
The joy of God's creation, two beings made for prayer.

God's humble heart is spoken, as man is given all.
The creatures pass for naming, and God awaits the Fall.

The serpent slides through Eden, with curses in his heart.
He tempts and lures the couple; God and man are torn apart.

But Love sees through the ages, for a second Man is planned.
And though man falls from glory; he falls not from God's hands.

In a manger meek and lowly, God sends forth his dear Son
A second Man arises; God's will, it will be done.

God walks veiled in man's image, and to free man from his sins,
He bleeds and dies for sinners; and majestic Victory wins.

Then God through death brings glory; and foils Evil's plans.
For even through the chaos, God has a sovereign plan.

And so through blood and death and life, man and God can dance.
And sacrifice that paid the price brings forth sacred romance.

THE MADRAS CAT

The madras cat blinked at me and said,
"You look purrrfectly fine, my dear,
Except for your skirt and your old wrinkled shirt
But meooow dear you have nothing to fear."

"For if purrrty is as purrrty does,
Your scuffed up shoes won't matter.
And the perrrrilous state of the hair on your pate
Will never be noticed I'd gather."

"So please, go to the ball," he said, preening his paws.
And he winced as he glanced my way.
"But don't dance with me, I'll be taking tea,"
He said, checking his bow tie and tail.

So I stroked the plaid neck of the madras cat
Then carried him out of the house.
And I went to the ball, shoes, hair, shirt, and all,
And I danced with the polka-dot mouse.

16

SELF-LOATHING AND THE LOVE OF GOD

Reflection 1

So God created man in his own image, in the image of God he created him; male and female he created them. Genesis 1:27 (ESV)

Meditate on what this means. Write a reflection about it.

Reflection 2

Blessed be the God and Father of our Lord Jesus Christ, who has blessed us in Christ with every spiritual blessing in the heavenly places, even as he chose us in him before the foundation of the world, that we should be holy and blameless before him. In love he predestined us for adoption to himself as sons through Jesus Christ, according to the purpose of his will, to the praise of his glorious grace, with which he has blessed us in the Beloved. Ephesians 1: 3-6 (ESV)

As you read these four verses—identify reasons you should NOT be filled with self-hatred but should instead see the beauty of God's love for you.

Reflection 3

*But you are a chosen race, **a royal priesthood, a holy nation, a people for his own possession,** that you may proclaim the excellencies of him who **called you out of darkness into his marvelous light**. Once you were not a people, **but now you are God's people;** once you had not received mercy, but **now you have received mercy.*** I Peter 2:9-10 (ESV)

Meditate on—don't skim-over the words in bold print. Worship and give thanks. Write a prayer of thanks.

Chapter II
MADNESS AND HOPE

O God, how filled with madness I have been at times! How lost. Alone. Gray and depressed—so filled with anxiety and fear I could hardly breathe. In those dark places, you seemed to disappear behind the fog of my mental haze. Your Word irritated me like fingers on a blackboard, abrasive to my heart. Worship was sand in my mouth and a sacrifice—bloody and dead. I mocked your promises with, "Whatever!" Faith was ridiculed by, "As if!" Prayer was a series of harassing doubts—faithless and futile.

But whispering, as a faint murmur in my heart, were the words, "To whom shall I go? You have the words of eternal life." I clung to that with bruised knuckles and broken nails.

I didn't like you much in those days. But you didn't seem to mind. You've never been afraid of me. You realized light would seep into the cracks of my wooden heart, and the fire of your steadfast love would melt the icy knot of fear and anger. You knew you'd prevail, and that your glory would press into my anguish and leave an imprint on my heart. An imprint that said, "Still mine."

I remember feeling like an angry two-year-old throwing a fit. Your arms bound me tightly to yourself to keep me from harm. "Why?" I'd scream, then kick, and you'd give no answer.

When fears encircled me and constricted like a serpent, hissing evil verses—leaving me gasping for breath, you were with me. When the cacophony of shrieking devils filled my ears, you whispered truth, a reality so sweet, I wept. You sang into my ear—holding me until I could finally feel your love and could hear your melody—a glorious song of hope.

You have been faithful. Thank you for your abundant kindness. For holding me in the icy darkness while you pierced pinholes and glimmered hope. Thank you for helping me chip away at lies, and for granting me eyes to see the deceiver. Thank you for the supernatural power of your Word, and how it brings faith and healing, courage and strength. Thank you for your faithful people who prayed, spoke, and encouraged me along the way.

I know I will experience blindness again. I've passed through it so often. However, I have grown to expect you to be on the other side of the closed door of my gloomy chamber. I've learned to put my ear against the splintered wood of the massive divide to listen. For you are there. You will be present in my future. This I know without a doubt.

CICADAS

My mind is full of madness.
Three a.m. and the cicadas
Roar in my head.
I run to catch them
And put them in glass jars to be seen and kept
Before they die when the next sun rises.

REASON FOR THE NIGHT

I can't see the logic or reason for night,
For when I shut my eyes, it puts sleeping to flight.

And though darkness may find me, my mind won't be still,
And Winkin and Nod will both pass as they sail.

And the Sand Man won't sand me, and stars will all jeer,
And the sheep will not jump or be counted I fear.

And the numbers I add in my head come to naught,
'Cause my thoughts won't calm down, and good sleep can't be
bought.

So then bury me now, and at least I'd find sleep,
And down six feet under I'd drift in the deep.

Then with Blinkin I'd float in a dark wooden shoe,
And we'd sail into night on a soft sea of dew.

BLACK INK

These melancholy words form in the darkness
And discharge from the tip of my pen like mad rivers
gorged from tears and clouds and
splashed like blood on the page
Black blood – un-trained to hope

P l e a d i n g   f o r   o r d e r
A n d   p   r o p er   sp a ci n g

Words of unbelief and fear

Confusion erupts and
            Drags me into hell

                Black words seep onto the page as if from another world

                I stare – amazed

THE DESCENT

"I will!" I shout. "I will go into that black grief
And cry until my soul has found relief."

I grab the demon of Despair
And leap headlong into thick black air
Struggling and moaning, gasping for breath,
Between deep sobs of infinite pain and death.
I land, a mass of broken care,
Prepared to be devoured alive by black Despair,
Who stands and towers proudly over me
And gloats and glimmers at his victory.

Laughing with a freedom born of love and power,
You flick him like a piece of dust from my funeral bower.
He shrieks and falls, grasping for a hold with all his might,
Hands still empty as his fingers clutch at light.

I sigh a wail of deep relief, collapsing in a shattered heap

To find I'm resting warmly in, the hollow of the loving hand
-----------of Sovereign glory.

BARREN

The trees stand erect in the cold winter air.
They sway ever gently as in some deep prayer.

Their boughs are now empty, and winter has come.
They stretch out their limbs as if reaching for home.

Their leaves have all fallen and lie on the ground.
It's gray and its drear everywhere all around.

But trees see brown leaves and remember the spring,
When life flows afresh, bringing life to dead things.

Trees weep not in grief, nor desperately grope,
But knowing the rhythm, stay rooted in hope.

I'M PLANTING A GARDEN

I'm planting a garden, a victory garden.
I'm sowing seeds of righteousness;
I'm pulling up roots of bitterness.
I'm planting a garden, a victory garden,
That I might bear fruit for my Lord.

He gives seed to the sower.
He gives rain to make it grow.
He gives sun to make it increase,
That we might bear fruit and abound to his glory.
He gives all that is needed,
Through the cross of Calvary.
That is why I'm planting a garden,
A garden of victory.

(Please read The Poet's Perspective on this poem.)

HOPE SOWS

When all of life is filled with barbs and weeds,
And only thorns and thistles seem to grow,
Hope puts on gloves, and picks up seeds,
And putting on a hat, begins to sow.

Hope takes a pick, and tends the rock-hard soil.
And gazing at the sky, he looks for rain.
And though he does not like the bitter toil,
He knows that future grace will yet sustain.

And though futility might seek to goad,
And tempt Hope to forget God's sweeter call.
Hope trusts that unseen hands will bear the load
And tend the soil when fainting he should fall.

Hope sees the grace that Despair cannot see,
And seeing it, works long within the field.
Hope views the garden as it yet may be,
And trusts that God through grace will make it yield.

MADNESS AND HOPE

Reflection 1

When my soul was embittered, when I was pricked in heart, I was brutish and ignorant; I was like a beast toward you. Nevertheless, I am continually with you; you hold my right hand. You guide me with your counsel, and afterward you will receive me to glory. Whom have I in heaven but you? And there is nothing on earth that I desire besides you. My flesh and my heart may fail, but God is the strength of my heart and my portion forever. Psalm 73:21-26 (ESV)

Guilt, anger, fear, lack of forgiveness, trials, and hatred can all embitter our hearts. What disquiets yours? How might the promises here help your emotions?

Reflection 2

Remember my affliction and my wanderings, the wormwood and the gall! My soul continually remembers it and is bowed down within me. But this I call to mind, and therefore I have hope: The steadfast love of the Lord never ceases; his mercies never come to an end; they are new every morning; great is your faithfulness. "The Lord is my portion," says my soul, "therefore I will hope in him." The Lord is good to those who wait for him, to the soul who seeks him. It is good that one should wait quietly for the salvation of the Lord. Lamentations 3: 19-26 (ESV)

Jeremiah, the Weeping Prophet, lives a life of tears. He has to prophecy disaster and watch it descend on his people. Waiting and hoping for God's faithfulness was a steady part of his journey. Meditate and imprint these promises on your heart. Let them give you hope. Take a moment to give thanks for his steadfast love in the midst of "wormwood and the gall."

Reflection 3

Therefore, since we have been justified by faith, we have peace with God through our Lord Jesus Christ. Through him we have also obtained access by faith into this grace in which we stand, and we rejoice in hope of the glory of God. Not only that, but we rejoice in our sufferings, knowing that suffering produces endurance, and endurance produces character, and character produces hope, and hope does not put us to shame, because God's love has been poured into our hearts through the Holy Spirit who has been given to us. Romans 5:1-5 (ESV)

Hope is present because of God's faithfulness, not our own. How does the idea that God is at work through your suffering make you feel? Hopeful? Angry? Weary? Can you find a measure of hope in it? Write about it.

THE DARK NIGHT OF THE SOUL

Many great saints throughout the centuries experience a deep sense of being abandoned by God. This is a link to an article about it. It should offer encouragement, especially if you happen to be passing through it. Spiritual malaise is a common experience among seeking, growing believers. If you are experiencing it, you are not alone.

https://www.soulshepherding.org/growing-through-a-dark-night-of-the-soul/

Chapter III

SIN AND FORGIVENESS

Father, I hated it when you showed me I was a depraved sinner. I knew I sinned often, and I knew I couldn't seem to escape the vortex of repeated failures, but when you showed me that I was like a piece of crystal that had fallen from the Empire State Building, broken in every way possible, it was more than I could stand. It seemed the worst news possible. The words "totally depraved" had somehow escaped me. I trusted you for salvation, but I didn't know how bad I was and what that actually meant. You had nothing to work with but my dead sin nature. I had nothing but your abundant love that would make you say, "She is worthy." I slipped into depression when it hit me.

When I recovered—after you had shown me the greater depths of your forgiveness and the power of your love—I wept. I wept because you knew everything about me and chose to love me—chose to save ME! You looked beyond my brokenness and saw beauty—an image bearer—a person, who, clothed in your righteousness and filled with YOUR Spirit—could bring glory to you and your holy name.

Thankfully, your love has never been dependent on my performance. Your affection has not rested on my acts of sinless perfection—for there are none.

And when you forgave, it was like no forgiveness I'd ever known. It was total acceptance—awareness that you made me new and had covered all my sin: past, present and future. Forgiveness meant freedom to walk in joy over my new identity in Christ: beloved daughter, friend, and bride. You loved me while I was your enemy. If you loved then, how much more do you love and forgive me now that I'm your child. This has become a source of incredible rejoicing! It makes me want to dance.

Now I see that the best thing you ever did for me was to show me my broken state. By seeing what **had** been forgiven and cleansed, I understood that you forgive today's sins, as well.

Thank you, Father, for sending your Son, for bringing truth and receiving the wrath that was due me. Thanks for convicting me of sin and convincing me of your love and forgiveness.

Thank you for showing me the depth of my sin and forgiving me willingly, wildly, and wholly. Your grace is truly amazing. I now have the righteousness of God in Christ. It's absolutely impossible! But so true! I LOVE YOU!

I SHALL REST IN YOUR MERCY

I shall rest in your mercy, Oh Lord.
That mercy that stretches far and wide,
From here to there,
The measureless length of your
Outstretched arms.
A mercy as deep as the wound in your side,
As fixed as the scars on your hands and feet.
I shall cease my work and rest.
For you are mighty to save.

SACRIFICE

Christ's blood is shed, and I am free.
Sin and shame – no hold on me.
I walk by faith and not by sight,
Trusting in your saving might.

And though I falter and I fail,
You, O God, you shall prevail.
The blood Christ shed for all my sin
Is effective.
And perfect.
It does work I cannot see.
It works its power,
And by your grace, covers me.

PETER'S SONG

The rooster crows; sounds fill the air
And would revive an old despair.
He seeks to raise an ancient shame—
The day that I denied your name.

Every day, I hear it call me,
Reminding me when I denied thee,
Reviving guilt, and dread, and shame,
Tempting me to deny your name.

Should I deny you once again?
Forgetting all you've done for men?
By casting shame, guilt, sin away,
On that dark and bloody day?

"Don't go there," your Spirit sings.
"I've set you free – given you wings.
Deny the shame – it is not yours.
Deny the grief – I've wiped your tears.

Deny the guilt of all your sin.
Deny your fear of sinful men.
But don't deny my blood or name.
Refuse the grief, fear, guilt, and shame."

So rooster, crow; crow day and night.
Your screech drives to the cross of Christ.
It sends me to his spear-torn side,
And in his blood-won grace abide.

CLEANING HOUSE

The sun stretches fingers to find me through the dust-filled air.
I pause and move my fingers down the dappled rays,
As if to stroke the brilliant threads
And pinch them between my fingers to pull the glory down.

I see dust in the light and light in the dust.

Curiosity bids me stare, and touch,
and steal one last glimpse—
Before the light fades
and the dust settles,

Or before I close the blinds.

WHATEVER THINGS WERE GAIN

Whatever things were gain to me I count but loss.
The righteousness found in my old flesh is chaff and dross.
But knowing you, is a value I can't express,
And to be found in you, your righteousness and nothing less.

I have nothing to bring to your holy throne but sin and shame.
And the promise I have in the blood of Christ and his Holy name.
So I stand here now, clothed in your beauty and grace,
And I know your sacrifice allows me to see your face.

Holy Lord, I long for you.
And nothing else will satisfy like you do.

Teach me to live every day in worship to your glorious grace,
Lifting all that I say and do as an act of praise.
In your debt am I, and I can never repay,
So I simply thank you Lord, now and every day.

SIN AND FORGIVENESS

Reflection 1

Have mercy on me, O God, because of your loyal love! Because of your great compassion, wipe away my rebellious acts! Wash away my wrongdoing! Cleanse me of my sin! For I am aware of my rebellious acts; I am forever conscious of my sin. Against you—you above all—I have sinned; I have done what is evil in your sight. So you are just when you confront me; you are right when you condemn me. Look, I was guilty of sin from birth, a sinner the moment my mother conceived me. Look, you desire integrity in the inner man; you want me to possess wisdom. Sprinkle me with water and I will be pure; wash me and I will be whiter than snow. Psalm 51:1-7 (NET)

David sinned against God with Bathsheba. Nathan had to show him his sin. Sense the depth of repentance. Go to the whole psalm if you like. Reflect on the last line. He sprinkles and cleanses.

Journal about your reflections.

Reflection 2

*For while we were still **helpless**, at the right time Christ died for **the ungodly**. (For rarely will anyone die for a righteous person, though for a good person perhaps someone might possibly dare to die.) But God demonstrates his own love for us, in that while we were **still sinners**, Christ died for us. Much more then, because we have now been declared righteous by his blood, we will be saved through him from God's wrath. For if while **we were enemies** we were reconciled to God through the death of his Son, how much more, since we have been reconciled, will we be saved by his life? Not only this, but we also rejoice in God through our Lord Jesus Christ, through whom we have now received this reconciliation.* Romans 5:6-11 (NET)

What was your situation before? (Look at the bold print.)

What did God do? (Look at the underlined print.)

What is it now?

Worship and give thanks.

Reflection 3

There is therefore now no condemnation for those who are in Christ Jesus. For the law of the life-giving Spirit in Christ Jesus has set you free from the law of sin and death. Romans 8:1-2 (NET)

Look back at the poem, "Peter's Song." Often the enemy speaks to us and accuses us of things for which we've already been forgiven. What would it look like to flip the accusations and turn them to praise for God's forgiveness? Can you imagine Peter using the words from Romans 8:1-2 against the accuser of the brethren? What would it look like for you to do that when he reminds you of ancient sin?

Chapter IV
PROFANE AND HOLY

Father, you see and know. You see my desolation when my flesh wins a battle or I partake of profane things—those evil, irreverent, or blasphemous things that darken my soul and create distance between us. When I do that, I walk away defiled for days, weeks, and sometimes years. I go into despair when I think of how unholy and contaminated I am compared to you.

But that's not where I need to land—in despair.

For though I fall short of your glory, your glory doesn't fall short of me. Your glory reaches into my heart, and as I behold you and see your beauty, character, and steadfast love, I am changed.

Change comes gradually—one glorious revelation upon another. One point of grace learned and believed. It is birthed through the conviction, confession, repentance, and forgiveness that follow each act of sin. It comes as I embrace your love and forgiveness and believe in the power of your presence in me.

I grow most when I'm fully aware that you are in me— longing to express yourself to this broken and incredibly hurting world. When I think of you living and loving through me, I am stirred to great hope! That is one of your deepest longings—your life in me—in your Church. You want your glory to pop out of me, unexpectedly—as I am captivated by YOU! And it does, surprising me, as well. Your kindness overwhelms me as you carve a place of holiness in my heart and dwell there, sweeping the shavings out the door into the darkness where they belong.

Please forgive me when I choose evil. Help me hate it with absolute hatred. Help me love you enough to abandon things that pollute me and see them for what they are, the "carrion of the damned." *

Thank you for the promise that you, who began a good work in me, will complete it. I rest on that. You gave your word. Do it, Lord. Whittle away at the profane, and dwell, holy and lovely, in me.

* Quote from "Ravenous."

RAVENOUS

I have sometimes filled my heart with profane things,
Things beneath Your worth and matchless name.
The world has lured me in to dine—
"Come eat the carrion of the damned."

I have drunk from muddy pools where vultures meet.
I've ripped with pointed teeth my share of flesh.
Chewed slowly. Swallowed. Stench upon my breath.
Impurity awakening evil appetites.

The bottomless urges cry for consummation.
How shall I quench my urgent thirst?

It won't be quenched, but like most longings— good or bad—
—once tasted and enjoyed—cry always and forever, "More!"

I'M IN GREAT NEED OF A CARPENTER'S SON

I'm in great need of a carpenter's son:
Someone who can lay his hands on wood,
And with drill and awl and a carving tool,
Make a lovely door or a resting stool.

Rough hands, with calluses and tiny wounds,
Accustomed to the splinter and the cut,
And tender with great power and gentle sighs,
A man with sweat and ache and piercing eyes.

He would not pause before a hardened oak,
But grasp it firmly, never letting go,
And work and work until his job was through.
There are no bounds to what his art could do.

For there's nothing too hard for such a one.
He is, after all, a carpenter's son.

SNOW DRIFTS

Kind and gentle, the snow falls,
Drifting into what is now.
A world of brown fallen leaves and winter bleakness.
Cold barren trees
Stand erect against gray sky and gathering snow.
White on black, black on white.
Snowflakes settle softly, coating all in purity,
Like holiness—slow and steady—soft and sure.
Truth by truth and step by step.
The earth welcomes the slowly growing blanket of clean, blinding whiteness.
So do I.
Come blanket my heart with holiness,
The slow and steady gift of your gentle and holy grace.
The invitation for your presence is open.
Drift in, oh Lord, and cover me.

THE PHOTO

The gloomy photo
Created in darkness and
Framed in shame
Stayed hidden at the bottom of my soul.
It stayed there in dark chemistry,
'Til it spit itself out – like a Polaroid Camera
But on speed and un-contained
It was:
Fire in my brain
Chest pain
Despair
And weeping, always weeping.
All because of some damned fool's libido and fiery lust,
And his slimy willingness to commit violence and penetrate my child-like soul.

UNFURLING

Do I believe that glory lies here? In me?
Somewhere in my heart? Hiding in the shadows
Of sin and disappointment, of un-lived dreams and un-spent
capital?

Do I believe I carry the nature of God?
Waiting to flower, urgent to bloom,
Tightly wound like a new bud, but swelling in sunlight?

Do I believe in God's power to set the bloom ablaze?
Stroking it with tenderness and igniting it with words of love and
hope.

Teach me to live from that part—the glorious, God-shaped part.
That holy sacred part—so stunning I could weep for its beauty.

Help me shed the icy frost, the safety of tightness, the security of
the known, the scent-less life of a green bud.

Help me say goodbye to the transitory cycle of my fading flower
and welcome the eternal bloom of your life in me.

Grant me eyes and will to live an unfurled life—a life bursting with
your glory and truth.

Open my eyes to the wonder of being wholly yours and embracing
your life in me, and watching you glow there—glorious, holy, true.

Open the hearts of others to their own God-shaped buds—waiting
in the silent shadows to bloom.

Give us all the joy of unfurling.

PROFANE AND HOLY

Reflection 1

We are all like one who is unclean, all our so-called righteous acts are like a menstrual rag in your sight. We all wither like a leaf; our sins carry us away like the wind. Isaiah 64:6 (NET)

Do you believe that? That your sins look like that? The poem "Ravenous" was intentionally graphic. When you read it, how did it make you feel? Reflect and write.

Reflection 2

I will sprinkle you with pure water and you will be clean from all your impurities. I will purify you from all your idols. I will give you a new heart, and I will put a new spirit within you. I will remove the heart of stone from your body and give you a heart of flesh. I will put my Spirit within you; I will take the initiative and you will obey my statutes and carefully observe my regulations. Ezekiel 36:25-27 (NET)

Reflect and write.

Reflection 3

Blessed is the God and Father of our Lord Jesus Christ, who has blessed us with every spiritual blessing in the heavenly realms in Christ. For he chose us in Christ before the foundation of the world that we may be holy and unblemished in his sight in love. He did this by predestining us to adoption as his sons through Jesus Christ, according to the pleasure of his will— to the praise of the glory of his grace that he has freely bestowed on us in his dearly loved Son. In him we have redemption through his blood, the forgiveness of our trespasses, according to the riches of his grace. Ephesians 1:3-7 (NET)

God gives us an imputed holiness. He transforms us over time with a genuine, walked-out righteousness. All of us fail to be holy. Give thanks for his steady forgiveness when you are profane, and repent boldly, trusting him to transform you—body and soul.

Chapter Five
DOUBT AND FAITH

Father, I guess my biggest doubt has always been that you could do something with ME. Transforming a lump of clay into a useful vessel seemed more impossible than the creation of heaven and earth. At least that's how it felt. I knew my weaknesses; they were legion. I knew my faithlessness and poverty of spirit. That usually led me to despair.

I recall how you first breathed the truth of your Fatherhood over me. How I began to see and believe that you were indeed my Father. Your love was greater, your faithfulness stronger, your forgiveness more complete than a human could ever conceive, much less earn.

Your Word says that faith comes by hearing and hearing by the Word of God. When I could do little else, I have been faithful to put your Word before me—even when I have doubted you and questioned whether or not the whole thing was even true. I planted your Word in my heart. I worshiped you when I didn't like you. Your Spirit has done what you have promised. Faith has come. Inch by obedient, and sometimes disobedient, inch.

I questioned, and still do, whether tomorrow will be taken care of. Whether I will have the emotional resources to handle future pain and suffering. I doubt you will bring my children home, that I hear your voice, that you are good, and that your character is spotless.

But you urge me to come, taste, and see that you are indeed good. Studying your nature helps me. Reading books by and about other saints and their journeys offers me wisdom. Having friends and pastors point to you when I can't see you is another thing you do for me. With every lesson, some of the veil is removed. My doubt becomes faith. And the whole time you place your hands around my face and say—"Can you see me now?" Both of us long to be seen and known.

You know every part of me. The problem with my doubt and faith is that I don't know you. Father, Jesus knew you completely and trusted in your goodness all the way to the cross. That's the kind of seeing and knowing that I want. When he knelt, he knew. When he spoke, he had heard from you first. O God, that I might know you like Jesus knew you.

But, I don't think I know what I ask for.

Still. I hunger. I thirst.

LIVING LARGE

Living small exhausts.
I WANT!
Large living
Large joy
Large love
Large faith to make
Large sacrifice and
Large friendships overflowing out and up and down.

SHOW ME!
Rivers, not streams
Mountains, not hills
Galaxies, not stars
Show me a big God
who sees beyond the sorrows and does not despair.
Show me a deep God
whose mind and thoughts I cannot know.
Show me a wide God
whose broad expanse catches the remains of the day
and brings them whole and healed into another.

I want no flaccid faith, no limp love.

I WANT!
The impossible, so that I might keep
Bent knees and
Blessed self-forgetfulness,
With all being found in Your High-ness.

DESPERATION

I gaze at the desperation of my soul – the dark places where I dare not look--

My lack of love, and a compassion so shallow that it does not move me to go beyond myself.

I question the power of your Spirit.

Is this faith in which I say I live real?

Am I in Christ?

Has the Spirit empowered me?

I feel so void of the resplendent and the divine.

My selfishness seems to be the only reflection that I see.

I am yours – save me!

Daddy God - Brother Jesus - fill me and do in me that which I am too weak to do myself.

NO STONES IN THE BASKET

There are no stones in the basket,
Only baked loaves, brown and sweet.
He brings me these gifts every morning,
But sometimes I don't even eat.

And day after day at my doorstep,
Is grace, love, and kindness for me.
They're wrapped in a basket of mercy,
Giving my hungry heart meat.

And seeking an answer to suffering,
And crying aloud in my pain,
Is not answered with serpents or mocking,
But love's sweet and tender refrain.

And so, I will cry unto you Lord,
With hope, as I seek your kind face,
And trust that a basket of mercy
Will be filled once again with your grace.

DOWNSIDE BACKWARD DAY

Have you ever lost your foundness
On a day that's upside down?
And the trees are gazing side-ward
At a sun that's on the ground?

And who and what you are is gone
And drifts upon the wind?
And your very favorite person
Seems more like a distant friend?

And you don't know where to find things?
And all's adrift and free?
And life has lost its moorings
On a rough and callous sea?

To regain a sense of foundness,
You must know you've lost your way,
And go baaing and go bleating
On your downside backward day.

And the shepherd will come searching,
And in the strangeness ride,
And you'll lose your sense of lostness
In the foundness by His side.

ODE TO THE WAVERING MOON

Oh waxing waning moon, I am like you.
One day I'm bright and clear with sparkling hue.
Some days will pass and I am drear and small,
And by all eyes that see, not seen at all.

The sun, resplendent, moves across the blue,
An orb of glory staying ever true—
The brightness constant, blazing on its own,
Unlike its little friend, inconstant moon.

The moon is so dependent on the sun,
And wishes she could be as that dear one,
Who warms the earth and fills the day with light,
But though she tries, might will not make it right.

So, little moon, stay fixed on that bright ball,
And though you waver, yielding to the fall,
And are hidden by some shadow on sun's face,
Or maybe you just turn from sun's bright grace.

Remember it's the sun who brings the glow,
And do remember, cycles come and go,
And you'll return, reflecting what you see.
With sun's help, moon will be what moon should be.

THE PLOT THICKENS

Supposedly there is a storyline
That weaves a thread amidst our darkest grief.
It's making sense of all the tears and pain,
And granting in the seeing deep relief.

I cannot see the plot or find the thief
Who steals away my hope and flees away,
And leaves me there to suffer unbelief,
And all is dark, though others say it's day.

And dare I try to dream you'll turn the gray
Into a story of redeeming grace?
And all have said that I should simply pray,
And trust that in the night you still embrace.

And you are weaving beauty edged in lace,
And though I see you not - my hiding place?

HOLLOW

I'm hollow. The others got to see.
He stood in their midst and spoke – or so they said.
But I was off on some fool's errand.
We were like
Rats those dark days – hiding in corners.
Death had come and our band of men would surely cave.
The Master was – dead – buried – I saw it all.
And when I heard them speak of what they saw – I swore that only
Touching with my eyes and hands would satisfy my unbelieving heart.

And everyone waited, hoping for another desperate journey into madness –
For so it seemed to me – this vision of the impossible.
And they re-lived how each had felt, what was seen
And it drove me wild.
I had no tale to tell and nothing to fill the fissure formed when he died.
The image of his crowned, bent, and bloody head and his severed body seared my soul.
The metallic scent of HIS blood had been all consuming.
Death had been absolute.
I feared hope.
I would not hope.

Then He appeared.
A mystery in white.
My flesh prickled.
I gasped, eyes wide in unbelief.

It could not be.
Life restored to that ripped, red, and ravaged flesh?
It couldn't be.

"Peace," he said.

My heart turned violently - spinning wildly between hope and disbelief.

"Be," he said.

The voice thundered with my pulse in my ears.

"With you." The words breathed gently onto me.

Me, the doubter. The cynic. The hopeless.

And He met me as I was.

Needing to use my eyes, not just my ears, to believe.

I fell; my legs no longer sure,

Shaking, weeping, joyful, stricken.

Driven to the madness of seeing the living dead -

This totally Other Man

Who stood before me as a wounded risen Lamb.

JUST SING

They wake and sing your praises
As the sunlight touches them.
Each bird creates a new song,
As the night lifts up its hem.

The cloak of darkness falls to earth.
The birds' songs fill the sky.
I hold my breath to hear it.
Do birds e'er wonder why?

Why babies fall from cozy nests?
Or wings break while in flight?
Why winter's icy breath still blasts?
Or it's dark, so dark at night?

No! Each just wakens to the dawn
And opens up its mouth.
Then sings of all your glory
To the east, north, west, and south!

DOUBT AND FAITH

Reflection 1

Jesus answered them and said, "Truly, truly, I say to you, you seek Me, not because you saw signs, but because you ate of the loaves and were filled. Do not work for the food which perishes, but for the food which endures to eternal life, which the Son of Man will give to you, for on Him the Father, God, has set His seal." Therefore they said to Him, "What shall we do, so that we may work the works of God?" Jesus answered and said to them, "This is the work of God, that you believe in Him whom He has sent." John 6: 26-29 (NASB)

The work of God is to believe in Christ and all that he has done for you: his steadfast love, absolute righteousness given to you, infinite mercy, boundless grace, every spiritual blessing, and free access to the Father. Meditate on just one of those gifts and give thanks.

Reflection 2

Then he said to Thomas, "Put your finger here, and examine my hands. Extend your hand and put it into my side. Do not continue in your unbelief, but believe." John 20:27 (NET)

Look back on the poem "Hollow." Christ is very tender toward this doubter. Place yourself in Thomas's shoes—in the place where you are full of doubt. See Jesus inviting you to touch him—his side, his hands, his feet. Acknowledge your doubt and accept his grace.

Reflection 3

And he said (of his demon possessed son)*, "From childhood. It has often thrown him into fire or water to destroy him. But if you are able to do anything, have compassion on us and help us." Then Jesus said to him, "'If you are able?' All things are possible for the one who believes." Immediately the father of the boy cried out and said, "I believe; help my unbelief!"* (Parenthesis mine) Mark 9:21b-24 (NET)

"If you are able?" Where do you need help with unbelief? What did Jesus do in spite of this father's unbelief? Cry out for help. Recall that Jesus gives good gifts.

Chapter VI

WRESTLING AND REST

Lord, how many times have I fought with you and wrestled over things I didn't like? I've been angry, sad, disappointed, and screamed in my fury, "I'll show you!" As if my arm could win against yours? As if my pathetic strength and will could out-distance the living God?

I've wanted my way and been miserable. I've up-ended my faith to spite your face. I've turned my back on you, even though you sought me with tender, persistent love. I have, like Jacob, wrestled, but you keep winning, and I'm glad. You've put my hip out of joint more than once as I've fought against you and despised your plans. Thankfully, I eventually settle into restless peace.

Longing for more joy, more life, more of you, I always wrestle. But as I write this, I'm reminded that the whole time that I fight, you attempt to give me gifts. Those gifts come in broken pottery and unpolished urns. But when I finally bow my head and receive them from your outstretched hands, I find they contain healing ointments and food for my journey.

While here—on this side of death—I imagine that all rest will be sprinkled with wrestling. We were made for wholeness with you, and until that day comes, we long for the more of what we still lack—holiness, beauty, perfect love, and un-cloudy days. No more tears.

Till then—I will find what rest I can, as I trust in you. Your Word teaches that Israel could not enter into rest because of unbelief. Teach me to have faith in your character and faithfulness. Trusting. Yielding. Believing that you are good—even though things might not look that way in my life or the lives of those around me.

Lord, help me redefine good as anything that comes from your hands—which is all of life.

Remind me that when I wrestle, I am, in that very act, clinging to you. Help me trust in your goodness, and in that position of faith, enter your rest.

10^{10}

I woke – and sweat was trickling from my face.
You'd pinned me to the ground yet one more time.
How often have I failed to win this match?
Each move outthought by you 10^{10} moves ahead.

Yet every time I try and try again,
As if my strength could win a victory
From one who lifts the planets, moves the sun,
And runs with joy throughout the universe.

Recovering – upon the floor I lay.
Cross-legged, smilingly, you wait for me.
Knowing that I'll try again once more
To try and wrangle grace out of your hand.

The irony of all the sweat and tears
Is that the thing I fight for, you have done.
By faith alone all of your grace is mine,
And what I seek to wrest from you, you give.

BIG HANDS

Your hands must be big
Because they hold all the prayers of the universe
          And sort and plant them like fine seed.
Crazy, conflicting petitions
each claiming rights to Your benediction.
Prayers spoken in haste
          Without your view from the heavens
Pleadings from hearts that do not comprehend
your glory or essence
Only seeing those things which can be seen
by the light of gray.

JOB'S SONG

In my complaint, I sought to fault Another.
In my pain, I wanted to place blame.
But across the chasm of space,
I heard the Sovereign Lord speak
And here's what He said, He said to me.

"Where were you, when I laid the earth's foundations?
Where were you, when I set the gates of the sea?
Have you ever commanded the morning
Or caused the dawn to know its place?
In all of these things, where were you?"

"Where were you, when the stars dripped from my fingers?
Where were you when I bent to create man?
And when the sun sprang from my womb,
And I held the earth in my hand,
In all of these things, where were you?

Have you plunged into the depths of the sea?
Do you know where the gates of hell may be found?
Do you know where the light dwells?
Can you lead forth the stars by name?
In all of these things, where were you?

Where were you, when I planned for your salvation?
Where were you, when my tears and blood ran like rain?
Where were you when my heart was crushed
Beneath the world's deepest sins?
In all of these things where were you?

To hear such knowledge of you is too great for me.
I cover my lips in shame afraid to speak.
For in all your glory and splendor, I find all I can say is,
"I find no fault, no fault in Thee! I find no fault, no fault in Thee!
And I bow unto you on my knees!"

O GLORIOUS FOE!

O, Glorious Foe! Come kill me with your love
       Those parts of me that need to die,
The parts that strut and preen and live a lie,
O Glorious Foe! Come capture me.

O, Glorious Foe! Wound me with your delight,
       Though I war and storm against you.
Do not cease until you win the fight.
Please storm the fortress that is called my heart.

All the fear – the fighting to be more,
       That comes from me and not from you,
O let me be a captive of your grace.
Bind me and chain me in your triumphant march.

If I run – please track me down.
If I should hide – please search me out.
If I should raise a weapon to my cause,
Disarm me with your redeeming love.

I will not stop 'til I am yours alone –
       And you command my every thought and deed.
Please kill my fear, my boasting and my striving –
O Glorious Foe, please fight and capture me!
O Son of God, come fight and capture me!

STORMY

The wind and the seas crash around you.
You rest in the stern of the boat.
Waves rise, and they fall at your bidding.
Faith keeping disciples afloat.

And you sleep as if lying on beaches,
Sun drenched and awash in God's love.
And deep calls to deep at your presence,
Seas calm at your voice when you call.

And he who commanded the weather,
Placed his life in the hands of a storm,
Of wicked and cruel intentions,
And let the storm beat upon him.

And rested three days while the storm raged,
In the palm of God's faithful hand,
Trusting through death's seeming triumph,
In a powerful omniscient plan.

And three days of torment and questions
Were stilled when God displayed His power.
Christ rose, and he vanquished death's raging,
Brought hope to the world in that hour.

PEARL

Perhaps I'll sleep when the Pearl comes,
And darkness is shoved to the horizon and flipped over the edge.
Light will be my resting place,
And I will sleep unsheltered and fearless,
For as long as I need.

SHEPHERD'S LOVE

The little lamb is nestled firmly in his Shepherd's arms.
The lion, wolf, and thief have ceased to cause him any harm.

Before his legs were broken, he had wandered far away.
The wolf had almost killed him; Shepherd entered in the fray.

The healing from the wounds took time, and Shepherd was quite
kind,
But once again the lamb was off; he had a stubborn mind.

The lion once had stalked him when he took a separate path.
But Shepherd smote the roaring lion – a token of his wrath.

Trembling from the fear he knew, he ran back to the fold.
But Shepherd knew this little lamb would be one he must hold.

The lamb's small legs were broken, in tender love so pure.
Then Shepherd gently carried him until his legs were cured.

When finally, the lamb was placed back on the grassy field,
He'd learned to love the Shepherd's voice and to it gently yield.

And during those long weeks and months, the lamb had ceased to
wrestle.
He'd learned to love the Shepherd's arms; he learned instead to
nestle.

THE YOKE

Take my yoke upon you; it is easy; it is light.
Please, stop your cold resistance; please cease your constant fight.

My goal is not to harm you or to cause you ceaseless pain.
My heart is but to woo you into great, eternal gain.

What makes the oxen stubborn, or what fear lies deep within?
Why such resistance from him and where hides his blinding sin?

What makes the oxen shy away? Why can't he yield his will?
Afraid the yoke will harm him, he refuses to be still.

Please woo my stubborn heart, oh Lord. Please love me till I rest
Beneath your yoke of faithful love and lean quietly – on your breast.

Reflection 1

He gives strength to those who are tired; to the ones who lack power, he gives renewed energy. Even youths get tired and weary; even strong young men clumsily stumble. But those who wait for the Lord's help find renewed strength; they rise up as if they had eagles' wings, they run without growing weary, they walk without getting tired. Isaiah 40:29-31 (NET)

What is the one requirement to find strength, according to this verse? Why "wait?"

Reflection 2

Come to me, all you who are weary and burdened, and I will give you rest. Take my yoke on you and learn from me, because I am gentle and humble in heart, and you will find rest for your souls. For my yoke is easy to bear, and my load is not hard to carry." Matthew 11:28-30 (NET)

What an invitation! Often God's yoke has felt very heavy—then I realize I'm trying to carry it by myself. Being yoked to Christ is not an invitation to heavy labor—it's an invitation to have someone stronger lift the greatest portion. In what situation does the yoke you carry need to be laid on HIM?

Reflection 3

Then, because so many people were coming and going that they did not even have a chance to eat, he said to them, "Come with me by yourselves to a quiet place and get some rest." Mark 6:31 (NIV)

Read and re-read this one verse. Write what you see about Jesus in this. Give thanks.

Chapter VII

DARKNESS AND BEAUTY

Father, when you created the earth, it was beautiful. It was good. I imagine all the angels watched in awe as you spoke the universe into existence. I love looking for those stunning things in your creation and writing about them. But sometimes I get stuck in the less-than-lovely things I see everyday.

I don't like the ugliness in the world—the sin-sorrow, the hate-anger, the body-sickness and the general brokenness and decay of this fallen world. I know it's part of the Fall, but I must say—I look forward to the day when all of that is gone. I look forward to ultimate healing and removal of all things that defile our world as a result of sin. I look forward to the completion of what you did at Calvary.

Father, I confess I don't know how to be balanced. I can chew on bad things and overlook the beauty—but I can also be guilty of overlooking the sorrows to protect my heart from the pain in the world.

Teach me the balance. Tutor me to see the sorrow but look beyond it to know the redemption you have for the world. In you there is hope for restoration. Help me be a servant of restoration and beauty—offering those things to the world in the form of love, truth, hope, and faith—as well as a glass of water, a word of kindness, and an act of mercy. I also ask you to keep my heart from the deep malaise of un-hope. Of seeing the sorrows and allowing them to bury me so that I end up being useless to your glorious cause of redemption.

So, help me seek the beauty in the ugly places around me. Give me eyes to spot the light in the shadows and to see the glistening loveliness of unnatural giving and kindness. Help me see the splendor in nature and live in a state of thanksgiving and praise because of it. But also stir my heart to offer redemption and light into the dark, broken places in the world.

THE DAYLIGHT SLIPS AWAY

Daylight slips away without a sound.
Into another's breaking dawn he steals.
And verdant shades of green he leaves behind.
As muddy browns of earth, their fragrance yield.

The grey-hued boughs release their pungent shades.
As Dusk looks back, a golden mist he makes.
A hazy glow now lingers on the lawn,
A bouquet in the wonder of his wake.

The air is densely charged with Dusk's fair charms.
Longing for more, I reach to make him stay.
But like a lover sighing sweet farewells,
He whispers to my eyes and moves away.

Dusk has come and gone and here I rest,
An afterglow of worship in my breast.

SHANGHAIED

My fears arise from your forgetfulness
The memories of thirty-thousand days
Forgotten
Shanghaied from the edge of reason by biology and chemistry.
Sorrow smacked me as I gazed at your bent gray head, stooped shoulders
Once laughing lips
Made limp by life's cruel strokes.
Is there dignity in this dark forgetfulness?

I fear the grief of memories snatched away

Holes – where memories once lay.
Will the one who suckled me recall my name?
Will the one who greeted my first breath with songs of joy
Remember?
Who I am?

Or yet, will I one day so slip away that I won't know the face of one I love and say,
"Aha, 'tis you, my love."

SEASONED

A little old lady and a little old man
Walk the shoreline hand in hand.
They toddle some (age has its signs),
But love and hands stay intertwined.
They inch along the turquoise sea,
These age old lovers – he and she.

VELVET NIGHT

Black velvet sky is pierced with little holes.
As glory glitters through each tiny tear.
The fingers of the night wake up the wind.
And in the balm of darkness stroke my hair.

The moonlight kisses leaves and tender lips.
An owl enchants the woods with its soft who.
Its hooting casts a spell around my mind,
And puts me in a trance of misty dew.

BLUE BIRD BYE-BYE

The wind was gentle when the blue bird came.
It perched then nested there – on that limb.
I saw it day after day.
It provoked me so - all perfect in its domicile.
It hatched then fed its young with bugs and worms.
I often sat beneath the tree
And watched her wild in her flitting.
Such a mother never was.
While sitting still and silent in the shade,
A young one fell near me.
The mother frantic, wild - urged me to flee.
Stepping to the fallen tuft
I looked at Mom, then bent my head
To see the babe
Then swiftly broke its neck and ate it raw.

Signed,

The Cat

SET

He had a studio
for making art
Right there in the darkness
of his home
Invited to observe
He closed the door
My soul like film took on an image
As he dipped and dipped.
A photo emerged
My soul was set
Right in the darkness
Of my friendless world
At six

GALAXIES

The stars shifted in the bucket as he tipped them out.
Shaking them gently, he released them from his pail.
They floated with a sigh across deep space,
Puddling in clusters throughout the universe.
The Maker blew, and galaxies began to twirl,
Moving outward with his gentlest breath.
He roared with joy,
The heavens shook.
Whirligigs sparkled and spun across the skies –
Vast space between each spinning coil.
Laughter again.
A cartwheel or two.
And it was good.

MYSTERIES

Don't let me refuse to taste of your mysterious ways -
The strangeness of your tender love, and how you rule my days.

How waves that pound the sun-lit shores and echo over land,
Declare your glory and your grace, and your determined hand.

The God that sent his Son in love, sent him forth to die.
And when the curse has bent me down, you long to hear my cry.

The bitter dregs and fragrant wines are intertwined as one.
And sovereign power and boundless love are summed up in your
Son.

DARKNESS AND BEAUTY

Reflection 1

If I were to fly away on the wings of the dawn, and settle down on the other side of the sea, even there your hand would guide me, your right hand would grab hold of me. If I were to say, "Certainly the darkness will cover me, and the light will turn to night all around me," even the darkness is not too dark for you to see, and the night is as bright as day; darkness and light are the same to you. Psalm 139: 9-12 (NET)

Meditate on and write about these verses. How can this be?

Reflection 2

I create the light and make the darkness. I send good times and bad times. I, the LORD, am the one who does these things. "Open up, O heavens, and pour out your righteousness. Let the earth open wide so salvation and righteousness can sprout up together. I, the LORD, created them. Isaiah 45:7-8 (NLT)

This is hard but true. Believing in God's goodness when evil is present is the greatest challenge to my faith. Re-read "Mysteries." Wrestle. Rest. Trust.

Reflection 3

The Word gave life to everything that was created, and his life brought light to everyone. The light shines in the darkness, and the darkness can never extinguish it. John 1:4-5 (NLT)

Read and re-read this. Write a prayer. Give thanks.

Chapter VIII
SORROW AND COMFORT

Father, you see this world we live in and understand our pain. We inflict wounds on one another's lives, and the natural decay and eventual death of each of us haunt our lives and taint the beauty of your created world.

But here we are. Sorrowful. Angry. Wistful. Longing for what hasn't yet come. Still you offer comfort in our affliction—the comfort of your presence and the presence of your people. You give us comfort in Scripture and in the promise of eternal life. You tell us that our suffering has a purpose. That as we find comfort, we can comfort others in similar ways.

We'd prefer the pain to be gone, but this, at least, gives purpose to our sorrows.

I am grateful for your Spirit who is called the Comforter. I can imagine you with me in my distress. I see your hand on a fevered brow and the bent head of my mother whose ravaged mind left her senseless. I see tears wiped away. Tenderness offered. I grieve. You give comfort.

But we, being made in your image are to give comfort, too. We are to be your presence to the weeping, the grieving, and to those whose pain we don't understand but see. It's a balm we offer—water, hands, a touch, or a prayer.

We comfort like we have been comforted by you—and it will have to be enough…until you return.

CLICK

Today began with sterile halls and white coats
Unexpected - poignant
Punctuated by pain and humble giving
Wiping her face and gifting water like honey to her mouth
She spoke small, drugged words and phrases
"I love you so much, Mother," she mumbled
Unconscious words rise, blessing those who've passed
Still, she loves and says so
Over and over again
(The heart beats on)
The machine clicked - dripping life and hope

MELANIE—UPON HER DEATH

It's but a gentle step from here to there.
A lifting up, a smile, a loving power.

And like the light of dawn you softly rise,
Full of strength with love bright in your eyes.

Taken by a hand, you mount the stairs,
Healed and whole, an answer to our prayers.

Your shell is left behind on sterile sheets.
You dance in beams of light on golden streets.

DEBBIE

She walks with stately form and grace
Grief's tears run softly down her face.

With eyes held high and lifted up,
She raises hands and empty cup

And then He comes as springs of wine.
(She is the branch; He is the vine.)

And pours his grace in liquid fire
Filling all her heart's desire

With hope and joy and love.

I AM NOT DEAD

I am not dead; I am alive.
Pain is the proof, and sorrow confirms it's so.
My tears deny the all-consuming lie
That I have rotted into dust,
And that the wind is blowing me away.

WHEN THE LIGHTS WENT OUT

Do you recall when the lights went out and the mask of death fell over unseeing eyes?

When the mind was snatched and the specter appeared?

When evil carried love into darkness and there seemed to be no cure?

And the tears fell in torrents, and joy rarely peeped over the edge of hope?

I do.

I was there – not healing yet – but offering My presence – My shoulder as a rest for your sobbing – My hand to hold you up.

Do you recall how you learned to trust there? In the place of darkness where My glory still dwells?

Do you remember how you dared to look into an unknown future where I AM?

How you pegged down the edges of your faith as a tent in a storm and dared evil to blow you away?

I do.

And when the next storm blows, you will find Me there again, helping you secure the pegs of hope and building your faith. I will be there as a place of rest and strength. And you will remain faithful, for I will teach you how.

For the unknown is not unknown to Me. It is clear and wide and filled with hope and faith and love,

For I am present there.

THE PHOENIX

The winds came and etched the surface of the earth,
Fingers on the hand of God.
We don't know why they came,
But they made furrows in the dirt and carved ruts
Where houses used to stand.

But now the Church rises, and
From his mouth he calls.
From cinder, rubble, and debris It moves.
Bubbling, roiling to life like a Phoenix,
Spreading wide its wings, it soars,
Seeing ruin, and weeping while in flight.

Drop by drop the tears of God now fall
And heal in gentle rain.

MAD LOVE

Grieve not for me, my friends; grieve not.

For today I stand on mountain peaks with Glory by my side.

Grieve not – but enter into my rejoicing.

My reward has come – my joy begun.

Celebrate my new life of un-blemished vistas, un-cloudy skies

Un-hindered mad love, and un-bridled worship.

Weep for yourself – if you must – that you must remain

And wait until it's your time to attend the feast.

Weep for yourself – if you must – that you can taste but partial joy,

And partial love, and see but a partial vision of God.

Weep if you must – for babes born and pray that they

Can taste the true, sure but incomplete grace of earth.

Grieve not for me, but enter into my rejoicing.

My hope is satisfied, for today I dance on mountain peaks

With Glory by my side, and I sing my mad-love to the Joy of Heaven.

And He sings his mad love to me.

SORROW AND COMFORT

Reflection 1

Blessed is the God and Father of our Lord Jesus Christ, the Father of mercies and God of all comfort, who comforts us in all our troubles so that we may be able to comfort those experiencing any trouble with the comfort with which we ourselves are comforted by God. For just as the sufferings of Christ overflow toward us, so also our comfort through Christ overflows to you. II Cor. 1:3-5 (NET)

Can the knowledge that God will make Kingdom use of our suffering give us comfort? Write about it.

Reflection 2

Even when I must walk through the darkest valley, I fear no danger, for you are with me; your rod and your staff reassure me. Psalm 23:4 (NET)

How do his rod and staff reassure and comfort you?

Reflection 3

Re-read "Mad Love." How does knowledge of your eternal life grant comfort now? In affliction? In pain? In emotional distress?

Chapter IX
FEAR AND COURAGE

O God, of all your creatures, I believe I am the most fearful. I've had to wage war against it. I've wrestled to believe you, and more often than I would like, have fallen prey to anxiety and dread. They've held me hostage in a prison of unbelief. Periodically, I'd snatch a key from my captor's belt and escape briefly, only to return again. It takes so much strength to combat this demon and the sin of unbelief.

You've watched me cross swords with panic and anxiety. You've seen me plunge into despair when I lost, and all light seemed to flee away. You've seen the demons chase me and watched as I've turned on them with you in me and by my side. We—you and I—have spoken truth into the darkness where bony hands reach to grab me and secure my seemingly inert life. You've given courage to fight, the will to live, and the ability to hope in your unfailing love. You've let me see beauty and helped me choose holy, brave things.

I've failed so often, I could sink thinking about it. Others were hurt by my wild fistfights with the nebulous shadows of fear. My children and husband have watched me fail and fall victim to fear and depression.

They've lived in my melancholy world where hope did not flourish, and I harmed them, Lord. I HATE it, but I can't undo it. I trust you to help them fight their own demons—partly introduced by me.

Believing you, knowing you, and trusting you with my todays and my tomorrows is a steady fight. But the more I truly know you, the more prepared I am for a brawl with fear.

Thank you for the courage you've given me through multiple streams of wisdom. The Holy Spirit gives me insight and strength to stay in the battle and live in my gifts and calling, as I attempt to live a life of courage and faith.

Thank you for running with me into the roar of the lion.

GET BACK IN YOUR HOLE

"Get back in your hole,"
I heard the darkness say.
"It's safe there for your soul.
Run, hide there from the fray."

"It's hard out in the battle,
And people are unkind.
They do not care about you
Or the warfare in your mind."

"Run and flee to darkness.
Close the door and hide.
Flee from discontented hearts.
There's no one on your side."

But Jesus runs to meet me,
With gentle healing power.
He binds my bleeding wounds and says,
"I've brought you to this hour."

"When you're insulted, you are blessed,
When cursed, you're glorified.
Go love, forgive, and be like me.
Live life now crucified."

"My way may seem like it is hard,
But light is warm and free.
Let go of what is binding you.
Let go and come with me."

DENIAL

Denial is:

That place I go to tally the good and subtract the bad until I can live with the total.

The telescope I use to make troubles appear smaller by looking through the wrong end of truth.

The book I read which causes the trials around me to fade behind the mist of a good story.

The memory lapses that occur when I buy something I shouldn't because God is calling me to do something more uncomfortable – like thinking of others.

Avoiding prayer by talking to a different friend.

Avoiding God's Word because it would mean conviction – and right now, I don't want that.

Exercising my body when my soul needs it more - or exercising my soul when my body is going to ruin.

Filling my time and space with anything but that which I need most – God.

Forging ahead when a still small voice is saying, "Be still and know that I am God."

Saying I'm fine when it just ain't so.

Not being concerned when my words, my heart, and my actions don't agree.

Believing I am more like my words than my heart and deeds.

Feeling despair for sin when a Savior has already absolved it and conquered it.

Remaining unequipped when the God of the universe has promised me so much more.

Not trusting the finished work of Christ to empower me to overcome my sin and failures.

Not believing God indwells me and is working in me for his glory and my good.

IF I KNEW I WAS BELOVED

If I knew I was beloved,
I know that I would laugh!
I'd pray believing faith-filled prayers,
And dance along my path.

I'd be a mighty witness!
I'd be a hidden saint.
I'd weep with deep compassion,
And rest with those who faint.

In all I said and all I did
His glory'd be my goal,
Whether wiping dirty bottoms
Or teaching thirsty souls.

I'd paint the Sistine Chapel,
And put flowers in a vase.
I'd pen the great Messiah,
And speak boldly of your grace.

If I knew I was beloved,
How hopeful I would be.
I'd know my steps were guided,
And see your hand on me.

When sorrows overcame me,
Like Jesus, I would cry.
Like Jesus, I'd be angry, too.
And in sweet faith, I'd die.

I'd imitate my Savior,
And do what that might mean.
I'd walk as He has made me,
Whether hidden, heard, or seen.

SEA SONG

The song begins with cerulean beat.
Mocking poems' iambic feet.
The sound of turquoise striking beach,
While white foam dampens as they meet.

The sunlight shimmers 'neath the sound,
Of blue-green rumble all around.
It asks me to wild faith be bound,
And getting lost in it, be found.

The vastness of the majesty,
Of things I know but cannot see,
To lose control in mystery,
And ride the rhythm of the sea.

THE POET

I see you standing there
Proud and humble
As you
Boast in the sacred work
With quiet words
Born of vanquished heart and desperate hope
Words that speak of promise and sunlit days to come
Of word joy and brave assault

THE HOURGLASS RUNS DRY

The hourglass runs dry as sand dives fast.
In joy the crystals plunge in bright cascade.
They know full well their moments do not last.
Each joy-light floats but seconds then it fades.

I wish to stem the flow of rushing sands.
They will not stop or linger as they play.
I seek to staunch the grains with wrinkled hands.
I give commands, but they go on their way.

And so, I bend my knees to unkind rules.
Of birth and life and pain and certain death.
And though sand flows, I will not be a fool,
But each day choose to leap with hope-filled breath.

Arms spread with grace-full heart head lifted high,
I'll dive, because the hourglass runs dry.

A PAINTER CAME

A painter came by stealth last night and painted all the trees.
He edged each bough with crystal and dripped white on fallen
leaves.

It did not take him long, I think, to scatter paint around.
But, my! He left it everywhere. And some he dripped in mounds.

If I had pulled my paint brush and with wild abandon, free,
Had left paint splatters all around, then shame, yes shame on me!

But he sneaks in on breezes, and mocks the canvas size,
And with exquisite tenderness paints all that fills my eyes.

FEAR AND COURAGE

Reflection 1

God is our refuge and strength, a very present help in trouble. Therefore we will not fear though the earth gives way, though the mountains be moved into the heart of the sea, though its waters roar and foam, though the mountains tremble at its swelling. Selah. Psalm 46:1-3 (ESV)

"The Lord is my light and my salvation—whom shall I fear? The Lord is the stronghold of my life—of whom shall I be afraid?" Psalm 27:1 (NIV)

Meditate on these verses and write about what God shows you about fear and courage.

Reflection 2

"Do not worry about your life, what you will eat; or about your body, what you will wear. Life is more than food, and the body more than clothes. Consider the ravens: They do not sow or reap, they have no storeroom or barn; yet God feeds them. And how much more valuable you are than birds! Who of you by worrying can add a single hour to his life? Since you cannot do this very little thing, why do you worry about the rest?" Luke 12:22-26 (NIV)

As you read this, are there words that stand out? Thoughts that especially resonate? Write them out.

Reflection 3

So do not fear, for I am with you; do not be dismayed, for I am your God. I will strengthen you and help you; I will uphold you with my righteous right hand." Isaiah 41:10 (NIV)

How does the fact that God is with you impact your fear and courage?

Chapter X
TEARS AND LAUGHTER

Papa, I love to laugh. After all, a merry heart is good medicine. I guess I cherish laughter so much because it's hard-won. I love the way you teach me joy. You've sprinkled mirth across the surface of my life as I've learned to laugh at myself, probably one of the healthiest things I've ever learned. I chuckle at how seriously I take myself. At how foolish I can be. I love delighting in your faithfulness to this melancholy child. You are amazing!

I think of Sarah, who gave birth to "laughter" (Isaac). She laughed when you told her she would have a baby, and she laughed even harder when a child was born at her old age. Everyone else laughed, too. If "laughter" (Isaac) is a type of Christ, then perhaps being in Christ also means that I dwell in laughter. For of all the beings in the universe, you have to be most joyful. You laugh at your enemies and the future. You laugh at our pride. "If you knew me," you say, "you'd realize your pride and laugh, too!"

You also say you grieve. We know you wept over Lazarus. You are acquainted with grief and a man of sorrows (Isaiah 53). In Hosea you grieve over Israel: "How can I give you up, O Ephraim?…My heart is turned over within Me, and My compassions are kindled." (Hosea 11:8 NASB)

I don't like tears as much as I like laughter. But tears are a sign that my heart is alive, and that I haven't numbed myself to pain and suffering. Tears mean I have sympathy and empathy with others, and that I still hate injustice and evil and the sorrows caused by broken humanity. Weeping also prompts me to go looking for joy and beauty.

So we have tears and laughter, like you. Thank you for both, but I admit that I look forward to the day when there are no more tears, and all the grief over this broken, fallen world is over. On that day, I will enter the not-yet I've been waiting for, and it becomes the forever "now."

Until then, Father, keep me laughing in my tears, and weeping in my happiness until you take me home.

LONGINGS

I long for You – to know Your pain – to be in empathy
To note the things upon which Your eyes rest
In love, or ire, or tender sympathy.

I long for You – to be so gripped – with who You are
That I would ne'er be overcome by anything
Save Your unfailing love and power.

I long for You – to break my heart – that I might see
The things in me that keep my feet
From following ever nearer unto Thee.

I long for Thee – as Moses longed – do not, I pray,
Take me from here unless
You swear to come with me along the way.

I seek Your face – as bride for Groom – each glimpse too brief
And every thought of You is fine and sweet,
And due to longing, bent to grief.

I long for Thee – to feel despair for sin – the sweet malaise
For deep, un-covered darkness
Which too oft' my heart and will embrace.

I long for Thee!
Help me, Lord, or I shall yet abide in deadly peace.

THE EYES OF THE LORD

The orphaned child, black and fat, with limbs like strings and teeth like pearls

> Came to my house last night on the wings of Technicolor sorrow and satellite TV —

Heralded first by a romantic comedy about rich and glamorous models in New York City.

I cried, then left her presence to proudly decry the cruelty of man and the ravages of sin —

> And to gaze at my indifference and affluence in shame.

My brothers and sisters died today upon the thin pages of newsprint —

> Murdered, I believe by hatred dark and blood stained hands.

The announcement came between an ad for Italian shoes and the society page.

> I burned with self-righteous anger then tossed the requiem of their deaths into my tidy, stainless, kitchen can.

I read from my Mac a tale of Aids,

> Consuming life, and hope, and strength 'til all that's left is black despair

On Yahoo I saw them frail and sick—small ones who look with hollow eyes for hands to help and hold.

Tallying the grief, I sighed with indifferent pity — the damage too great – for me to amend,

> I felt the pain but briefly – ever so briefly – lest I weep and weep and weep again.

Filled with the liberty of your grace, I rejoice in your unfailing love and faithfulness —

> At least for me. But what of these? To what second hell will they repose?

I close my ears and dance and sing – loudly - to shut out the noise

Thankfully, the world glides silently by - screaming at the top of its voice —

    Who will come and deliver us from our tormenters?

    I smile ... and wave.

Where is the Body who believes that Christ has...

    Forgiven our sin, Granted the Spirit,

        Made us righteous, adopted us as His very own,

            Set us apart to glorify His name,

Equipped us with all things needed for righteousness and godliness,

        Called us to go into the world to preach, to teach, to make disciples,

            Given us faith, shown us our Father,

Placed us in union with Himself, wrapped us in His love,

        Sent us on a mission, promised us eternal life.

          Where is the Church Triumphant?
           Where am I?

I asked you, Lord,

    to show me the things upon which your eyes rest in love, or ire, or tender sympathy.

        I am filled with shame... and grief... and unbelief..........

But God .... through Christ,

    Still whispers hope - of promised death and

        Vibrant-Life, and Oneness joined in union sweet

          To be his eyes, heart, hands, and feet.

ENOUGH, I'VE HAD ENOUGH

"Enough, I've had enough
Of deadly peace."
In love, you kissed my heart with deepest grief.

"Enough, I've had enough
Of idol bliss."
In love, you gave me loss and sorrow's kiss.

"Enough, I've had enough
Of selfish gain."
In love, you filled my heart with others' pain.

"Enough, I've had enough
Of un-lived power."
In love, you welcomed me into your funeral bower.

"Enough, already!" now I cry.
"Please cease the sorrow, or I'll die!"

"I can't," He says, "My Word I gave.
But, I'll wrap you in love while we're here in the grave.
And in death's embrace, you'll find me there
With peace, and bliss, and gain, and power."

AW SHUCKS!

Aw shucks! Floating ducks! Muckity mucks. Men in tux.
Diaper pails. Pale ales. Yellow hay in giant bales. Piggy tails.
Fluffy skirts. Words that hurt. Children playing in the dirt. Little
flirts.
Daffodils. Whippoorwills. Ghostly chills. Sleeping pills.
Perspiration. Agitation. Word navigation. Inspiration.

A PARODY OF "A BIRD CAME DOWN THE WALK" BY EMILY DICKINSON

A BOY CAME DOWN THE WALK

A boy came down the walk,
He did not see me there.
He snuck behind a bush to pee,
And sprinkled in the air.

He drank a Mountain Dew
From a frosty mug,
Then sat beneath a big oak tree
And squashed a juicy bug.

He glanced with impish eyes
That worried all around.
Then pulling out a cigarette,
He smoked, then threw it down.

As one in laughter, taken,
I offered him a smile.
Then uncorking lanky legs,
He ran at least a mile

Or two if I could know it.
I mustn't see his game.
On flying feet he fled me.
I never knew his name.

CADENCE CALLS
(TO BE READ LIKE A JODY CALL)

Lo I hear the trumpets' sound
Raising saints up off the ground.
Up they're flyin' one by one,
Leavin' earth goin' toward the Son.
Sound off, one two, three four.

There goes one head bent in prayer.
Up he shoots strait in the air.
Left and right like birds in flight.
Oh my Lord it's such a sight!
Sound off, one two, three four.

Naked, dressed, and eatin' bread,
Wakened, risen from the dead,
Shakin' graves and rattlin' bones,
Crashin' cars and splittin' stones,
Sound off, one two, three four.

The Captain's cadence echoes wide,
Callin' saints to the other side!
Countless millions here they come!
Marchin' upward headed home!
Sound off, one two, three four!

A Jody Call is a marching chant you might see and hear if you
watch a movie about soldiers and war or if you are present during
training exercises on a military base. Soldiers chant in rhythm with
the march. Some chants are bawdy, some are meant to encourage,
and some are just silly and meant to lighten the load of training.

AMBROSIA

Too much.

I filled my cup in excess yesterday and drank of heady words too often.

The drunken hangover fogs my brain – but

There was humor here – I remember.

Somewhere.

I swear it's so.

But I will not repent of my drunkenness or of the

Cramp-belly laughter,

Sore-cheek laughter,

Hiccough laughter,

  Burp and giggle laughter,

Silly, over-the-top, bare-bottom-baby laughter.

I must confess.

I indulged in witty decadence, and gluttony of the soul.

  I swilled champagne words and guzzled fermented language.

I tasted deep-dark-chocolate-liqueur humor.

I was drunk and intoxicated - inebriated by potent wit and clever potions.

But I will not repent.

There was no sin – I only drank the nectar of the gods.

THIRSTY

I've run till all that's left of me is ash.
Then lying in the dust I pant and wheeze,
And dreams of water spin around my head.
I hope for that and then a scrap of bread.

I gather to a well to find my hope,
A drink, a swig, a gulp of life.
And there I'll wait till someone comes
With bucket, rope,
And opposable thumbs.

The Dog

TEARS AND LAUGHTER

Reflection 1

You will make known to me the path of life; In Your presence is fullness of joy; In Your right hand there are pleasures forever. Psalm 16:11 (NASB)

Is your God joyful or is he an always-serious deity who never laughs? The psalmist says that in his presence is fullness of joy. How do you see him?

Reflection 2

For His anger is but for a moment, His favor is for a lifetime; Weeping may last for the night, But a shout of joy comes in the morning. Psalm 30:5 (NASB)

Most of us have passed through seasons of tears and laughter. Does the idea that "this too shall pass" bring you hope? Do you believe he will be present in your future?

Reflection 3

You have taken account of my wanderings; Put my tears in Your bottle. Are they not in Your book? Then my enemies will turn back in the day when I call; This I know, that God is for me. In God, whose word I praise, In the Lord, whose word I praise, In God I have put my trust, I shall not be afraid. What can man do to me? Psalm 56:8-11 (NASB)

God puts tears in a bottle. This imagery lets us know that God is tenderly disposed toward our sorrows. Reflect on this verse and these sentiments. Underline words that mean something to you.

Chapter XI
BUSYNESS AND STILLNESS

Father, you know me. You know how I can become unsettled in my slavish need for approval and acceptance. You know how my "yeses" can exceed my minutes. How I can rush headlong into a quagmire of commitments—which ultimately drain my life and keep me from wisdom and peace.

It seems I dash between the two: busyness, that ultimately drives me to solitude and stillness, and then isolation that drives me toward busyness.

I love it best when your Holy Spirit prompts my activity, and from that position of love and peace, I move toward others. I don't like it when my bustle is based on some warped sense of personal need or a false paradigm where I believe I can actually fix a situation.

O Holy Trinity, I enjoy so very much the time I spend in stillness with you—the moments when I sit on my porch and listen to the birds in the morning and smell brewing coffee and the morning air—crisp and fresh. I love how stillness cocoons me in wonder and I can sense your embrace there. In those moments, worship becomes my highway to you and the pleasures you hold— for in your presence is fullness of joy and in your right hand there are pleasures forever (Psalm 16:11 (NASB)).

Thank you for the times you call me to stillness—silence— solitude. In those moments I feel like I'm on a date with you. We are visiting—like two friends. I'm enjoying you—you, my Creator, God, and Father. You, who are my Savior and Redeemer. And of course, I'm delighting in your precious Holy Spirit who is your steady indwelling presence in my life.

But I also sense that you are delighting in your child—me. The righteous me—who has received my righteousness by your hand alone. O God—how I love you!

Please mature me so that all my busyness grows from my time with you in stillness, and please teach me to find moments of refreshment when busyness is unavoidable. Help me practice being in your presence, Lord.

WAITING

From all those things that seek to snare me,
From all the paths that lead my heart astray,
From all the lies that seek to bind me,
Be still my soul, and in the silence stay.

With no plans but waiting on you Lord,
And knowing you long to embrace us
With loving kindness and tender mercies.
We lift our hearts and eyes and in you trust.

So come, O Spirit, come, and let us see
The glories of your endless wonder.
O God, we have, we have no strength but thee.
O God, we have, we have no strength but thee.
Be still my soul, and wait for Christ alone.

KABODING

Have you ever gone kaboding by fireflies in June,
While the silver breezes whisper in the light?
Have you witnessed stars in chorus singing praise in velvet night,
Lullabying all those gazing at the moon?

And the scents of honeysuckles rise as soft as a caress.
Leaves shiver in delight in whispering winds.
A distant owl whoos gently, singing songs to long lost friends,
Hoping in great peace some soul to bless.

Kaboding takes in sights and sounds and lifts them as a song.
It breathes and offers incense of the smells.
Kaboding lightens all our loads but heightens what we feel,
Brings thankfulness and straightens what seems wrong.

So, come kaboding with me, though I usually go alone.
Please come and see the things your heart might find.
And hide in fragrant wonder in the woods beneath some pines,
Then let the butterflies carry you home.

SILENCE – ALL YOU UNHOLY VOICES

Silence! All you unholy voices.
Quiet! All you loud clamoring calls.
The Lord my God deserves a word now.
I listen to him, properly enthralled.

The world shouts with proud and sure demands.
In a trance, I move with every beat.
Silence! I must listen to my Maker.
Like Mary, I will sit at Jesus's feet.

Be still oh steadfast inward spirit,
Even though the world shouts, screams, and jeers.
The Lord is in his Holy temple.
With quiet peace, to him I now draw near.

THE MUSIC OF SILENCE

Silence leads a symphony.
Deep forests sing in harmony.
Mountain peaks sing bass, and sigh.
Stars whisper a lullaby.

Bare trees, erect, carol in the snow,
Gaily clad in scarves of mistletoe.
Clouds, like divas, cross the sky,
Singing songs to heaven on high.

Creation hums together
As God's love so commands.
And God conducts the silence,
As only Holy can.

SILENCE

I sit beside silence – warm and soft,
Waiting for it to speak.
But silence never does.
It stretches out instead, and takes a nap,
On my new couch, and is at peace.

BUSYNESS AND STILLNESS

Reflection 1

Surely I have composed and quieted my soul; Like a weaned child rests against his mother, My soul is like a weaned child within me. Psalm 131:2 (NASB)

What a warm image of the Lord and us. Imagine it. Lean into Christ. Rest upon his breast. He is always present.

Reflection 2

For thus the Lord GOD, the Holy One of Israel, has said, "In repentance and rest you will be saved, In quietness and trust is your strength." But you were not willing, Isaiah 30:15 (NASB)

Cease striving and know that I am God; I will be exalted among the nations, I will be exalted in the earth. Psalm 46:10 (NASB)

Mediate on these two verses and write about them.

Reflection 3

The apostles gathered together with Jesus; and they reported to Him all that they had done and taught. And He said to them, "Come away by yourselves to a secluded place and rest a while." (For there were many people coming and going, and they did not even have time to eat.) They went away in the boat to a secluded place by themselves. Mark 6: 30-32 (NASB)

Put yourself in the frame. Imagine the chaos. Hear the invitation. Go with him to that secluded place.

Chapter XII
DEATH AND LIFE

Dearest Father, I'm sorry that we humans sinned against you and brought death into your glorious creation. I'm sorry that to save us from our awful error, your Son had to enter death so that we could have life. I thank you for loving us enough to deliver us from the curse of death and its fearful apparition. It looms over us as a skeletal reminder, but you have placed a new vision before us. Glory. Hope. Eternal love and joy.

The hope of eternal life brings buoyancy to my life. It raises me above the waves and keeps me from drowning in the pains of this present life of broken dreams, harsh cruelty, and sin-sorrow. Death, and the hope of eternal life, keep me grounded when I love this world too much and am enjoying its beauty, laughter, and love to excess.

And when I grieve, help me to remember the hope that is before me, before us, and help me faithfully offer that eternal hope to those who are on the sidelines of the race toward glory.

Thank you for the promise that you will help me persevere until that door of death opens for me. Please keep me from faltering, from failing, and from foolish paths. I want to finish the race well.

I look forward to life on the other side of the door of death. Having watched others pass through the threshold, I know that great suffering can happen before I go through the portal.

This would be my greatest prayer:

If my suffering is long, please preserve me and keep me ever saying, "Jesus," with such love, worship, and tenderness that I live on the edge of tears.

DOOR OF DEATH

For those who are set free from sin by faith in Jesus Christ,
A death is but an open door, that leads us into life.
The pain we suffer on this side, the fallen world we're in,
Cannot compare to glory or the joy we'll find in heav'n.

And passing through, we'll finally hear the closing of the door.
Then pain and sorrow melt away, and tears will be no more.
And as we see our Savior's face, our praises will not cease,
As all the fears we've left behind will transform into peace.

But to those who will stay behind and watch the closing door.
They grieve, but not as without hope in Christ their loved one's Lord.
And though there is a sorrow, that death has brought their way,
Rejoice that he who trusts in Christ stands whole in glorious day.

BORN ALOFT

I hate death.
Yet it is such a common thing.
And grief is so extremely ordinary – but should not be so.
Such raw emotion should have greater worth,
And sorrow should be born aloft instead,
And take flight upon the shimmering wings of angels,
And be held silently in the bosom of God until it has become his glory.

BREATH OF HEAVEN

I measure the moments by your breath
And the hours by the rise and fall of your chest.
The rhythm brings me rest,
But each breath is one less.
Each rise and fall of your chest is one closer to the final moment
When death shall be no more,
And all transfuses into life and light.
Oh, that I might lose my life in the rhythm of your breath,
and be taken away with you,
And be caught up in the Breath of Heaven and be one with Life.

WHEN THE SAINTS GO MARCHING IN

Will drums and trumpets be the sound
For saints to march toward heav'n?
What cadence will the Captain call
To soldiers freed from sin?

"Arise, the dawn is breaking loose!
The night is finally past!"
"Death's grip is finally shaken free!
For life has come at last!"

"The anxious can find sweet repose
Unbound from human fears.
Life and love now rule all things;
I wipe away all tears."

Adorned in white with glory kissed
The army marches home.
The fight, at last, is over now,
And victory has come.

The Captain's cadence call goes out
And saints toward heaven fly.
They march as one rejoicing throng
On highways through the sky.

SAILING

The boat close to a distant shore was lovely in the breeze.
I saw the billows swelling as it plowed the blue with ease.
I often caught a glimpse of it when others joined to ride,
And I gloried in the beauty of the boat upon the tide.

I sometimes even wished that I could be a traveler there,
Letting unfurled billows take me to the-who-knows-where.
I do not fear the boat or the trip across the sea,
But how I'm going to enter, is the thing that frightens me.

Will I board by stormy waters or in winter's icy gale?
Or be plucked out of the vomit of the belly of a whale?
Will I gently step into the boat from sugar-white, warm sand?
Or be dropped by helicopter to the beating of a band?

Until I board the boat to sail across Elysium's Sea,
I will waiver between fear and hope in what is planned for me.

I HAVE NO POWER HERE

I sit and watch you breathe – the up and down motion of your chest
Creating stillness in my own heart.
It moves in slight syncopation with the machine huffing beside you.
My breath joins with yours and holds us tightly, but
I have no power here.

I speak and sing, you breathe – the up and down motion of your chest
Creating stillness in my heart.
You receive blessings with eyes closed and mouth wide open.
My hand joins with yours and holds us tightly, but
I have no power here.

The end draws near – the breathing slows –
The stillness of my heart unbinds, barely held together by your fading breath.
It slowly loosens – then unravels wet and loud as you exhale one last time.
I hold your hand then kiss and wash your face with tears,
but breath is gone and nothing holds us tightly.
You see. I have no power here.
I have no power here.

DEATH'S DYING

Knees bending
Tears falling
Heart breaking
Blood dripping
Friends sleeping

Sun setting

Silver buying
Kiss betraying
Crowds lying
Lips denying
Whips lashing
Shoulders bearing
Hammers pounding
Flesh ripping
Body thirsting
Voice calling
Presence fading
Darkness falling
Heart failing
Sword piercing

Hopes dashing
Fears rising
Storm approaching
Faithful weeping
Faith sighing
Darkness blinding

Sunday's coming

Women walking
Spices wafting
Christ rising
Angels speaking
Women running
Mary sobbing
Gardener greeting
Joy swelling
Amazement filling
Hope living
Disciples laughing
Life bursting
Death's dying

I FIND I WANDER EASILY

There is a place I long to be ever closer unto thee.
I find I wander easily; please keep me ever close to thee.

Like Mary sitting at your feet, help me always faithful be.
I find I wander easily; please keep me ever close to Thee.

To hear the words and then obey, every word enchanting me.
I find I wander easily; please keep me ever close to Thee.

Be a lover to my soul, and sing a love song over me.
I find I wander easily; please keep me ever close to Thee.

The sirens sing, false lovers woo, stirring me to darkness flee.
I find I wander easily; please keep me ever close to Thee.

Drown all other songs and tunes, and keep me waltzing always free.
I find I wander easily; please keep me ever close to Thee.

MAY "JESUS" BE MY SIGH

I long to know you, Jesus
Like you knew the Father--
To feel your pulse, know your will
To be one with my Lover.

To abide in your Word,
'Til it becomes my breath,
To dwell in your love,
Until I pass through death.

I long to hear your laughter,
To dance on eagles' wings,
To soar the earth in worship,
To hear what angels sing.

I long to hold your hand
When Death is drawing nigh.
And if my mind has left me,
May "Jesus" be my sigh.

I long to burst through heaven's gates
And race to touch your face,
And be overwhelmed forever
By your beauty and your grace.

DEATH AND LIFE

Reflection 1

Be very careful, then, how you live—not as unwise but as wise, making the most of every opportunity, because the days are evil. Ephesians 5:15-16 (NASB)

We live, but we will die. The question is, "How shall we live?" Write a prayer to the Lord.

Reflection 2

Therefore if you have been raised up with Christ, keep seeking the things above, where Christ is, seated at the right hand of God. Set your mind on the things above, not on the things that are on earth. For you have died and your life is hidden with Christ in God. When Christ, who is our life, is revealed, then you also will be revealed with Him in glory. Colossians 3:1-4 (NASB)

These words seem impossible. Mediate on them. Write a prayer in response.

Reflection 3

This is eternal life, that they may know You, the only true God, and Jesus Christ whom You have sent. I glorified You on the earth, having accomplished the work which You have given Me to do. Now, Father, glorify Me together with Yourself, with the glory which I had with You before the world was. John 17:3-5 (NASB)

What is eternal life according to Christ? Does this impact your heart? If so, how?

Chapter XIII
WORSHIP

Dear Lord, part of me doesn't even want to introduce this set with prayer. The whole set IS prayer. But thanksgiving is always in order. Worship is always good. Thank you for teaching me to worship you. You led so gently, marking my resistance and fear with a smile and a nudge—you knew what my heart needed and longed for.

I remember the first time I lifted my hands in praise to you. I felt like a fool as I inched them up. But at one point—somewhere in between my waist and my shoulders, I was set free. I know you laughed with joy over my obedience. A dam broke. I obeyed what you said. "Your lovingkindness is better than life, My lips will praise You. So I will bless You as long as I live; I will lift up my hands in Your name."*

I entered a new phase of faith. Life was a mess; my husband was unemployed; we were living with my mother. Still, I was discovering that YOU are enough—that I could be satisfied with your faithful love. Before I knew it, I was running and leaping in the early mornings on the green rolling hills of a nearby golf course. I couldn't contain the wonder and joy of your faithful love and grace.

Exuberant! Amazed! Thrilled! The scales were falling off. My faith was no longer rules but relationship. Not law but life—a life that flowed through me and back out to you.

It hasn't stopped. There are seasons where worship ebbs—life, depression, sin, and grief might bring it to a pause, but with each new discovery of the riches of your grace lavished on us all, I return to uplifted hands, bent knees, song, and dance. Because you alone deserve all praise, glory, and honor.

I love you, Lord.

*Psalm 63:3-4 (NASB)

HELP OUR LIPS

Righteousness and holiness surround your glorious throne.
Righteousness and holiness belong to you alone.
In heaven all the voices cry holy, holy, holy.
Hearts respond and angels bow in humble praise before thee.

Not on earth can we dare hope to know your glorious ways.
Even we, though called your own, offer half-hearted praise.

Our hearts don't see your glory or behold your holy kingdom.
Our view of you is earthly-skewed with bright-eyed glimpses
seldom.
Open up our thankless hearts and fill our mouths with praise.
For you have given grace and grace and grace for all our days.

We gladly lift our poor-tuned voices singing as we can.
Honor Lord our frail attempts to worship One so grand.
Let our praises find an entrance to your holy throne,
And kindly let our hymns to you help make your glory known.

So on earth our hearts dare hope to know your glorious ways,
And may you kindly help our lips to offer worthy praise.

O GREAT AND AWESOME GOD AND KING

O, great and awesome God and King
Let earth and heaven with praises ring!
For you alone deserve such praise.
Therefore our loud Hosannas raise!

From dawn to dusk from east to west,
Let saints in adoration rest.
And everywhere and every place
Declare your love and boundless grace.

How excellent, how kind, how good
Is our risen Lord, our food!
Our drink, our hope, our life, our joy!
So, leap and sing and praise employ!

Spread his glories far and wide!
Tell it all and nothing hide!
His life, his death, his risen form,
His blood has made the dead re-born.

Day and night do not give rest!
But shout, and to his grace attest!
O sweetest joy that I should get
To bear his praise upon my lips!

COMMUNION SONG

See the Lamb of God – his nail pierced hands, his wounded side.
See the blood flow down from Jesus Christ the Crucified.
See his outstretched arms inviting all he calls to come.
See the love pour down, mingled with tears and sweat and blood.

See the risen Christ, the glory shining from his face.
Scars where blood did flow declare his mercy and his grace.
No one stands before the risen Lord in strength and pride.
All fall to their knees, and his mercy, seek to hide.

See our glorious God the blessed Father, Spirit, Son—
Eternal Dance of Glory – our God the Three-In-One.
Bow before his throne, breathe in his love, his power, his grace,
Then humbly rise and place a thankful kiss upon his face.

I OWE SO MUCH

I owe so much to your boundless mercy.
I owe such debt to your tender grace.
The depth of sin that you cleansed within
Humbles my heart, makes me bow my face.

Such holy love and matchless glory
Sent unto us in the form of man,
Causing our hearts to be silent before
Such a glorious God – such a humble plan.

You rob me of pride as I see your goodness.
I see no worth in my life but Christ.
My small acts of kindness and frail deeds of mercy
Are there because of the YOU in my life.

Dependent and helpless, a wee babe am I,
Unable to crawl to your pure throne of grace.
So lift me, I pray, in your strong arms of power,
And let me in thankfulness kiss your face.

FOR CHRIST ALONE

When dead in sin, God's mercy flowed
And put us in His Christ.
That he might show kindness and grace
And give us power for life.

Help us to walk in this kind truth:
That we're daughters and sons.
And help us live, as we're beloved,
For in Christ we are one.

Filled with the Spirit by your grace,
Please sanctify our hearts.
Without a spot or wrinkle be,
His glorious bride, the Church.

For we were darkness now we're light;
May we bear light's sweet fruit.
Trying to learn what pleases you--
All righteousness and truth.

To him be glory in the Church
And in his Christ forever.
For he has graced abundantly
And shared with us his power.

Inebriate our hearts dear Lord
And make us drunk with love.
And giving thanks and singing praise,
Live life for Christ alone!

WORSHIP

Reflection 1

Though the fig tree does not bud and there are no grapes on the vines, though the olive crop fails and the fields produce no food, though there are no sheep in the pen and no cattle in the stalls, yet I will rejoice in the Lord, I will be joyful in God my Savior. Habakkuk 3:17-18 (NASB)

This can be hard. Read. Meditate. Pray.

Reflection 2

For He rescued us from the domain of darkness, and transferred us to the kingdom of His beloved Son, in whom we have redemption, the forgiveness of sins. He is the image of the invisible God, the firstborn of all creation. For by Him all things were created, both in the heavens and on earth, visible and invisible, whether thrones or dominions or rulers or authorities—all things have been created through Him and for Him. He is before all things, and in Him all things hold together. He is also head of the body, the church; and He is the beginning, the firstborn from the dead, so that He Himself will come to have first place in everything. For it was the Father's good pleasure for all the fullness to dwell in Him, and through Him to reconcile all things to Himself, having made peace through the blood of His cross; through Him, I say, whether things on earth or things in heaven. Colossians 1:13-20 (NASB)

Read. Meditate. Worship. Write a prayer.

Reflection 3

Oh, the depth of the riches both of the wisdom and knowledge of God! How unsearchable are His judgments and unfathomable His ways! For who has known the mind of the Lord, or who became His counselor? Or who has first given to Him that it might be paid back to him again? For from Him and through Him and to Him are all things. To Him be the glory forever. Amen.
Romans 11:33-36 (NASB)

Worship in whatever way you want!

POET'S PERSPECTIVE

Chapter I
SELF LOATHING AND THE LOVE OF GOD

GOMER

Our pastor preached a series on Hosea. As he did, I was struck by God's persistent love for Israel as well as the Christian Church. I was reminded, too, of our resistance to his love. We don't understand it or believe it could be as good as it is. We doubt that his grace could cover our sin *and* us. We doubt grace alone would allow him to accept us. We can be filled with deep guilt or shame, or we think that the Christian life is boring or unfulfilling. Sometimes, we are angry because God hasn't answered our prayers. Like Gomer in this poem, we need to let him fold our hearts into his love and lose ourselves in his eyes. He loves us madly.

CREATOR'S PRAISE

On the road to being healed from self-loathing, I contemplated Scripture about being an image bearer—made in his image, fully and completely a child of God. Chosen. Loved. Blessed. It's hard for someone who hates oneself to believe. As I read, I was convicted because I often worship with wild abandon when I stand before natural wonders. The Lord spoke to my heart and asked me to stand before a mirror and look. Then he told me to worship him for making me. You see, I too am a natural marvel created for the glory of God. I worshiped in tear-filled wonder, for any human is superior to every mountain or sea.

MY PARADIGM—MY WORDS

I wrote this after listening to others' poetry, and I quickly realized that my style and my words are all I have. I am not another. I can't force myself to be what I am not. But I and my words matter, just as you and yours do. I only have my experience. I can learn other forms of expression, but I never have to imitate. Besides, writing poetry often exorcises the torments in my heart—thus the fine sweat cooling my body.

THE F-WORD

My journey into self-loathing began with childhood molestation and rape. During the process of being "seduced" and pursued, he used the "F" word repeatedly. I associate that word with evil. The act of marriage isn't supposed to be so sullied. I trudged through life with guilt and shame, and the event(s) distorted my self-image. It has taken a lifetime to trust that I am an image bearer and deeply, completely, and tenderly loved. So, I HATE the "F" word; it profanes the beauty of God's creation.

CRY ALOUD

I wrote this after meditating on the words of Christ in Matthew 7:7-11. Jesus talks about God the Father never giving us bad gifts. Sometimes, however, I don't believe God is good—especially when smacked by difficulty. But he is much more than I can envision, and his character is so unfathomable that if I saw him, my breath would be taken. My biggest regret is the years I didn't comprehend his goodness; I missed so much love and tenderness. It's like a bride who refuses to consummate a marriage, and then, when she finally does, she understands an important missing element and is filled with regret.

SACRED ROMANCE

This is the gospel story. Creation—the Fall—sovereignty—mercy—grace—redemption—salvation—restored relationship and romance. I wrote it as a Christmas card that I sent to friends. It was a reminder that the manger wasn't just the beginning of the great unraveling at the Fall. Restoration began before the Garden. It's a hard concept, but if believed, brings great hope.

THE MADRAS CAT

Why is this poem in a section on self-loathing? It's because I sometimes feel like the girl in the poem who is wearing an old wrinkled shirt, scuffed shoes, and is having a bad-hair day. I envisioned the madras cat being a madras stuffed animal. I actually dreamed the first two lines. When I awoke, the poem flowed. I think this is also about not listening to the derisions of others. When evil speaks to us—mocking us or acting condescendingly, we need to grab it by the scruff of the neck and toss it out the door and go to the dance—as we are. After all, we have been invited and we are deeply loved. And if you want to, dance with the polka dot mouse. I do.

Chapter II
MADNESS AND HOPE

CICADAS

It was another sleepless night. I wrote at least three poems that evening, including "Reason for the Night" and "Pearl." Fear and anxiety can keep me awake, but in this case, I had a mind full of ideas and thoughts—those were the cicadas. I wanted to capture them that evening, because ideas can have a short life—like a cicada—if not written down.

REASON FOR THE NIGHT

Insomnia—not my friend. But when it comes nowadays, I just go with it. I write, clean, read, and maybe, just maybe, doze off again. I wrote this and "Cicadas" the same night. It was a long night, if I recall. I distinctly remember being annoyed at my husband, who was snoring away while I penned poems on the floor at the foot of the bed.

BLACK INK

I wrote this during a season of severe depression. I usually had a heart of worship, but the sorrows that hit my life during that season were so many, I could barely lift my head. My disabled mother moved into our home, and she suffered from mental confusion and was angry about the move. My youngest son was impacted by her mean-spirited behavior toward him, and I grieved over his mistreatment. My oldest son denied his faith and chose to walk without God. My daughter was suffering deeply, and I couldn't help; I grieved and feared for her. Everything (including myself) felt hopeless. But God saw, and over time, led me from the darkness—but not on that particular day.

THE DESCENT

Emotional pain is horrible—worse than any physical pain I've ever experienced. This poem was during a season of deep despair, and I yielded to it—gave in—descended. But God surprised me there with a glimmer of hope. The pain didn't disappear as if by magic, but I knew God was present and holding me.

BARREN

Winter speaks of an unproductive season of life, but the seasons remind us that things are always changing. This harsh winter day will yield to sunshine and life in the spring and summer. I get a bit gray during winter seasons, but trees don't. They simply wait for spring to come and continue a life of unspoken praise.

I'M PLANTING A GARDEN

This poem seems a bit corny, but it means much to me. This little ditty has helped shape my life. I lay down one day to rest my feet while meditating on half a dozen verses about the sower sowing seed. Verses included Isaiah 55, Matthew 13, and II Corinthians 9. The words were coursing through my head and heart, along with John 1 and 6, which held the truth that the Word is life. I dozed off. I awakened from the nap singing this song. I had the words, melody, and all. I wrote it down, grabbed my guitar and marked the chords. It was so complete that I called friends and our music director. Had they heard it? They had not.

At the time, my heart was a garden of tangled weeds. I was taken over by sin, bitterness, anger, and fear. This song reminds me that I am responsible for planting the seeds: taking in God's truth, worshiping in community, praying, confessing, and repenting of sin. He, however, does the hidden work. His seed WILL bear fruit. He convicts of sin, gives power to his Word, sends confirming voices, waters his Word, even while we sleep, and he makes our small acts of faithfulness abound to his glory! He promises victory in our personal lives, and he assures us that he who began a good work in us will be faithful to complete it.

HOPE SOWS

Hope is one of those topics that isn't discussed often. It isn't quite "faith" and it isn't exactly "trust." It's a word filled with longing— unmet and not guaranteed—at least that's how it feels. Sometimes it hurts to hope. If we have faced multiple disappointments, it's even harder. But there are things we can hope in: God's faithfulness, his character, his promises, and the power of the Word to bear fruit. Hope urges us to keep moving. To never give up—to keep planting seed and trust that a harvest will come.

Chapter III
SIN AND FORGIVENESS

I SHALL REST IN YOUR MERCY

When beset by shame, I need to remind myself of God's mercy. The image of Christ's outstretched arms welcoming me into grace is one I often carry in my head and heart. The reminder of the price he paid and his willingness to pay it for me—for us—helps me to embrace forgiveness and hope. We must choose to rest there. We have no power to save ourselves. Our striving to earn salvation is worthless. Efforts to be good enough to earn Christ's love are arrogant and will always fall short. Our only safe choice is to receive what he has freely given.

SACRIFICE

As believers, we are constantly in need of the reminder that the blood of Christ does more than we imagine. This removal of shame is a theme that repeats itself often. It's a fight I engage in frequently. When I first understood mentally that I was forgiven so freely, I could scarcely believe it. I have to preach it to myself over and over again.

I don't remember exactly when I wrote this, but the words remind me of that frequent battle.

PETER'S SONG

I wrote this one Easter after church. Our pastor talked about the forgiveness available to Peter. I began to wonder what that looked like—how did he walk it out? How did he get rid of the shame he most surely felt after denying Christ? I imagine those days between Christ's death and resurrection were especially excruciating. It probably remained so until Christ took him aside to assure him—in a backward kind of way—that he still had plans for Peter and that Christ's love remained.

It probably wasn't until the Holy Spirit came that Peter actually got it. I thought of the daily reminder of a rooster's crow. It would probably have triggered old memories and brought back shame. But to walk in the fullness of God's mercy and forgiveness, Peter would need to let the daily crowing of the rooster stir up a reminder of the incredible forgiveness Christ purchased at the cross. The crowing, instead of shame, would be turned into a source of thankfulness. **"Oh, the incredible love and grace of**

God!" is something he might have shouted each morning when the rooster sang his harsh song.

To continue to embrace the shame meant denying the grace and love that God showed through the sacrifice of Christ. That would have been a second denial of Christ.

When trapped by sin, I need to remind myself that I've been forgiven. When life brings back a reminder of my shame, I can shout at the darkness—"Go ahead and revile me all you want. I've been forgiven, and sin and shame have no hold on me!"

To walk in my shame denies the power of the cross and the eternal gift of God through Christ. It denies God's work and is ultimately prideful. Instead, humility receives and rejoices, and stands amazed at God's good gifts.

CLEANING HOUSE

I remember where I was standing before I wrote this poem. At first, I sought to describe the light filtering through the dust I stirred up while cleaning. One thought led to another, and this was the result. "I see dust in the light and light in the dust," is the key phrase. Our sin shows up most clearly in God's light and truth, but we also see the light's rays because of the dust (our sin or pain). However, we can choose to close the blinds and see neither God's light nor our sin.

WHATEVER THINGS WERE GAIN

This was written as a song. It came after meditating on Paul's assertion that he counted all his life as loss compared to the true value of knowing Christ as Lord and of possessing Christ's righteousness instead of trying to establish his own.

The more I grow in an understanding of God's love, grace, and mercy, the more I see the chaff and dross of my efforts. I can agree with Paul.

I am utterly startled by the grace of God, and I'm forever grateful for his forgiveness and for giving me his righteousness, so I don't have to establish my own.

Chapter IV
PROFANE AND HOLY

RAVENOUS

I wanted to paint a picture of the extraordinary ugliness of sin. I don't believe that fact as often as I should. Sin encumbers us, weakens us, and creates fissures in our hearts that are difficult to fill.

Past sins impact today's decisions and the ability for me to resist new temptations.

We all have sinful inclinations, and we have our preferences for sin. We also judge the sins of others—theirs is worse than ours. But sin, when regularly yielded to, creates addictive behaviors. Whether it is sexual addiction, drugs, alcohol, excess computer or T.V. usage, or regularly yielding to anger or self-indulgence: our acquiescence can intensify our longings, but in the power of the Spirit, we find ourselves more capable of resisting.

The same can be said about our longings for Christ. Once we taste of him, our longings also intensify for him. If we feed our spiritual longings, they will intensify. If we feed our sin, it will gain power. What shall I be ravenous for today?

I'M IN GREAT NEED OF A CARPENTER'S SON

We are all rough-hewn pieces of chosen wood. God has plans for all of us. Often, I see my life as a splintery mess. But God lays gentle, firm hands upon me and begins his work— crooning songs of love and tenderness, helping me to bear the cutting and the carving. All the while, he's doing it with his own loving, nail-pierced hands—holy hands that didn't deserve the piercing or the wounding. He's imagining something greater than I can envision— something more beautiful than humanly possible.

What's most astonishing of all? He won't stop until the work is done and his vision is complete. This is true of all who are his.

SNOW DRIFTS

During a southern snowfall, I watched as the snow slowly gathered, flake by gentle flake. It was a quiet work. Un-relenting. Steady. That seems to be one of the ways God brings holiness into the darkness of our wintery, barren hearts. We can be unaware that it's even coming—especially if we place ourselves into situations that give us that opportunity—like prayer groups, Bible classes, communal and individual worship, and personal meditation. Conviction, repentance, and the power we need for change drift in, and we are slowly and steadily transformed.

THE PHOTO

I was raped as a young elementary-age little girl—age six to seven—it was a process. If you know me—don't imagine who it might be. You would be wrong. The perpetrator was a teenager (not a family member) who lured me into his basement, pretending to be my friend. He wanted to experiment and explore his sexual urges. He was filled with the raging hormones of puberty. I was longing for a friend. That excursion into evil transformed me—creating a fissure in my soul that has been hard to fill. Like most evil, it came on gradually. He convinced me of his friendship. I responded as one needing a friend.

Gradually, evilly, he warped my vulnerable, child-like heart and penetrated me—body and soul. It wasn't until I was an adult that I began to actually process the evil that was done. As a believer, I was taught to forgive, and I "had." But while working in a counseling office, I discovered that first I needed to admit to myself the depth of the evil that had actually been done. I shouldn't minimize the atrocity or its violence. As I dealt with this, I raged. I hated, and I was angry with God for not protecting me. I slid into deep depression and rage. These slowly abated as I truly forgave that misguided adolescent for the depth of the evil actually done. NO ONE should ever be subjected to the horrors of sexual abuse—especially young children. Predators should be prosecuted. Victims should be protected and given the opportunity to heal. If you are reading this and have experienced something similar—I pray you find freedom from the powerful impact of abuse.

UNFURLING

This is about the reality of sanctification and how it is possible because God dwells in me. If I am holy, it is because he is holy. I have no intrinsic holiness. But HIS glory is in me, waiting to be set free into the universe of broken lives, weary hearts, and decaying humanity so that he can bring hope and truth. It is love and beauty on steroids, waiting to be released into the world through his Church.

Chapter V
DOUBT AND FAITH

LIVING LARGE

I don't know about you, but I want big things. I want to KNOW God. Human understanding is watery when compared to the incomprehensible power and love of God. But—I still want to KNOW Christ. I would love to be sacrificial and filled with faith—all the time. But I don't, and I'm not. But Christ is kind; he says that we simply need a mustard-seed size faith. And that's about the size of it!

I believe I want these things for right reasons. I want to keep humble before his glory and be bound up tightly in self-forgetfulness. By knowing him deeply, I'd also KNOW that everything good in me is because of him. I want BIG things because I have a BIG God and this world desperately needs a big, big God and a big, believing, loving Church.

DESPERATION

Because I want to live large, when I don't see the fruit in my own life, I can be filled with despair. This was one of those moments when my weakness and sin felt like an undefeatable reality. But we belong to HIM. He is responsible for us.

One of my favorite scriptures is Psalm 119:94 (NASB): "I am yours, save me." That implies that I belong to God and he is ultimately responsible for maturing my soul. His Word also teaches that he began a good work and will perfect it. (Philippians 1:6)

My cry, "I am yours—save me!" is the cry of utter dependence in my weakness.

But on this particular day (and many others since)—I groped for faith and felt only my sin and the apparent reality of a life that was not particularly divine.

NO STONES IN THE BASKET

This poem came after meditating on the words in John about God not giving stones for bread or serpents if we ask for the Holy Spirit. The God of the universe brings grace every day to my doorstep. It is there for me. It is there to counsel, encourage, and help me. It is there to build me up and renew my faith for another day's need.

Occasionally, the hope of blessings found in God's Word felt false. Somehow, I thought that if I went to the Word or to him in prayer, he'd bring me despair for my sin, hopelessness for my efforts, and condemnation for my failures. But as I've come to know him, I see a kind face. Trouble, one of life's less-favored gifts, is always coming to us, in one form or another. But God is present with true comfort and wisdom, love and hope.

He never moves; we just don't always see him. His gifts are always good, and that can be hard to believe.

DOWNSIDE BACKWARD DAY

I am convinced that everyone faces moments of confusion, doubt, unbelief, and a sense of uncertainty about what to do next. Sometimes I experience that as a mental fog or an unencumbered flow of conflicting thoughts and ideas.

Some of the worst moments come as I believe Evil and his accusations. The words are filled with recrimination or paranoia. The accuser of the brethren is called that for a reason. He not only accuses us before the Father, but he also accuses us to one another. He will tell us, "He doesn't really like you. She doesn't think you are smart enough to… Your prayers don't matter. Who do you think you are?… Your life is worthless," and the words go on.

On those days, I need to hear the voice of truth. Truth and hope are anchors for our wandering hearts. And where do I go to hear that? I call out to the Shepherd of the Sheep with loud bleating and he comes and finds me with his Word. But sometimes, I have to call out for a while before I **see** that he is present. In reality, he's been there the whole time.

ODE TO THE WAVERING MOON

When challenged in a writing contest to write about the moon and contrast it in some way to the sun, I wrote this poem.

I invite you to think about the differences and compare the two. We are definitely more like the moon than the sun, and we depend on the "son" for our "glow."

THE PLOT THICKENS

Sometimes life seems like a series of disconnected, difficult occurrences. When I wrote this, that's how it was. People kept telling me that everything was going to be all right and that God would cause all things to work together for good. I wasn't fond of those words of "encouragement."

Many of the issues that led to this poem have remained unhealed. I have seen victory in other situations.

As I write this summary, I believe that God is indeed "weaving beauty edged in lace." But tomorrow, I might not. Something might happen, and that deep hope could vaporize by some errant doubt or fear.

However, I do know this: that if hope fades, I'll fight for faith. It's worth it.

HOLLOW

Occasionally, I practice Lectio Divina, or divine reading. In that practice, one reads and re-reads Scripture, and then meditates on it. When I did this through John 20, I imagined the scene when Jesus first appeared before his disciples and Thomas was absent. Then I imagined how it was when Thomas was there.

I tried to envision how Thomas felt before he was able to see Christ. He probably got tired of the disciples going on about having seen Jesus. The Scripture indicates that he had replied to the account of, "We have seen the Lord!" with the retort, "Unless I see the wounds from the nails in his hands, and put my hand into his side, I will never believe it!" (NET John 20:25, 26) I love that Christ took Thomas where he was—an unbelieving man—and offered his body to be touched and felt to allay doubts. That should reassure us doubters.

Christ's reply should also encourage those of us who have not seen but have believed—"Blessed are the people who have not seen and yet have believed." (John 20:29b)

JUST SING

Scripture says that all the earth praises God. The Book of Psalms speaks of creation singing the praises of the Lord. "Shout out praises to the Lord, all the earth!" "Let the rivers clap their hands! Let the mountains sing in unison before the Lord!" (Psalm 98:4,8 NET)

Their simple existence declares God's glory. All creation—without lips—speaks of God's power and sovereignty. Every movement, every flutter of wings, ever rustle of leaves can declare the glory of God if we listen. Creation does not doubt. You might say, "Of course it doesn't; it can't."

I guess that's my point. As God's unique creation, I don't want to doubt, even when "winter's icy breath still blasts." I want to "just sing," even if tears are flowing.

Chapter VI
WRESTLING AND REST

10^{10}

I imagined a wrestling mat, and Jesus was my sparring partner. He was stronger and was always able to know what I was going to do next. None of my moves caught him off guard. He always won.

When I say, "Cross-legged, smilingly you wait for me," I imagine him sitting on the mat and smiling at my impudence in thinking I might actually win a battle with him, but he's not too concerned about my efforts as I grasp for what I want.

I am a little like Jacob wrestling with God and saying, "I will not let you go unless you bless me." In my stubborn insistence for one thing or another, my hip can be "put out of joint."

I don't think wrestling with God is wrong. In those moments, we are still clinging to him and are staying in a relationship with him. He will win, and it's ultimately for my good.

That's the irony. I'm fighting for what I think I want, and he's already giving me an abundance of the things I need. I'm wrestling, but I really need to simply rest in his goodness and grace.

BIG HANDS

As believers, we pray. I've often been amused by the countless prayers that make their way into heaven's throne room and yet are in conflict with one another—especially at sporting events and during times of war.

The Sovereign Lord gets to sort all those prayers. I imagine he shakes his head occasionally and says, "They have no clue about who I really am or what they're asking for." Still, he keeps on sorting and answering according to his will and plans for mankind.

JOB'S SONG

Perhaps you are not like me. Maybe you are more like my husband who understands without question the sovereignty of God and his right to rule in any way he chooses. He was in the Army and understands authority. I, on the other hand, question it—then more than now. I'm always trying to think of a better way to do things.

Often I question God for having done things a certain way. During a season of tough questioning, I was led to read the last three chapters of Job. Much of this poem was taken directly from those chapters. I originally put it to music. The last verse was a bit of a bridge, so the meter is a little different from the rest of the poem.

O GLORIOUS FOE

Before attending a class reunion, I found myself desiring to be more than I really am. I wanted to make a statement, be somebody—this is a feeling that many who attend reunions can attest to. But there was also a desire to be my real self—the person who has had her life changed by Christ. Weak person that I am, I found old high-school demons rising from the dust of unlived dreams and false selves.

I didn't want to fall into old patterns of self-doubt. I wanted to be self-forgetful. I wanted to love rather than need to be loved or accepted. I made it through, but not without struggle. This poem is a cry for deliverance from myself.

STORMY

The main thought in my mind and heart as I wrote this was, "How does faith help me rest?"

I thought of Christ sleeping while the storm raged, and then I mulled over how Christ rested in his Father's love as he died and went to the grave—ultimately trusting that he would be raised from the dead.

Faith in the goodness, sovereignty, and power of God seems to be a key to rest. It helped Jesus rest as the winds blew the boat around. It also helped him be silent in front of Pilate's judgment seat and submit to the beatings of Roman soldiers. He rested in faith, in his Father and his plans—even though Jesus pled in submitted reverence for a different option.

There is a scene in the movie, *The Lion, the Witch, and the Wardrobe*, where Aslan lies down and lets the evil hoards tie him and drag him to the table for sacrifice. They shave and abuse him. He doesn't lift a paw or roar against them. He rests while they do their evil. He is sad, but he knows there is something deeper at work.

Perhaps trusting that God is doing a deeper work in our sorrow and suffering is also a key to rest in our storms.

PEARL

If I recall, it was another sleepless night—but this time I was worrying about something.

The Pearl is Christ. I will find a measure of rest on this side of glory—but real rest won't exist until I'm face to face with glory himself. At that time, darkness will go. Sin will be done with. My heart will be at peace.

SHEPHERD'S LOVE

I am a wrestler. I question God—sometimes—on many things. But God knows the danger of running away from his love and truth. He knows the sorrows of a prodigal child. Rather than allowing the lion or the wolf to capture me and devour me, he created a kind of brokenness in me that pressed me into his arms. My pain created a seeking heart.

This poem is about that struggle and the joy I began to experience as I let him carry me through my pain rather than resisting him because he "caused" it. Over time, I learned I'd rather nestle up close than go my own independent, unsafe way. I'd rather trust than doubt.

THE YOKE

During a particularly difficult period of adversity, I found myself resisting obedience and avoiding God and his Word. I knew better, but I feared obedience. Obedience felt like a heavy yoke—not like the one in Matthew 11:30 defined as light and easy. I knew I needed to know God's love more deeply so that I could yield more quickly, but all of life felt like death. This is a cry to God to woo me into obedience through his faithful love. Seeing God's Word as ONLY LAW can create resistance if you have never experienced the depths of God's grace and love—much like the oxen in this poem.

Chapter VII
DARKNESS AND BEAUTY

THE DAYLIGHT SLIPS AWAY

I watched the lawn from my sitting room window as the evening settled in. It was still, peaceful. While praising God for his stunning world, my heart was enraptured as I experienced worship and awe. I used mixed descriptions because sometimes as I observe the world, everything mingles together as one. Earth sings, dances, and gives off fragrance—all at the same time. Boughs release pungent shades. Dawn whispers to my eyes.

SHANGHAIED

My mother had a stroke, and I watched mournfully as her memories slipped away and her personality changed. It was beyond disturbing. I feared the day when she couldn't remember me or my name. That day eventually came. But this thoughtful watching created a different kind of fear in me: I knew the day might come to me, as well.

The thought of not remembering someone's importance or relevance in my life is alarming—as I'm sure it was for my mother. Slow decay is horrible and sad. But according to data, that is how most people exit this life. This is one of the things I dislike most about this fallen world. However, God has a plan to redeem. She was a believer, and on the other side of her forgetfulness, God provided eternal joy, complete healing, and a perfect mind.

SEASONED

Love is beautiful at any age. I watched two ancient lovers (probably in their late eighties) toddle along the edge of the sea. It was a tender sight. The poem is about what I saw, but it's also symbolic of how we need to walk through life—hand in hand with people we love.

VELVET NIGHT

I relish being still and observant in nature. I enjoy closing my eyes and sensing the breezes and listening to the sounds around me. There is a kind of acceptance within nature. It is what it is. There is romance, but not always. Observing and describing what I see is a joy to me. It makes me probe for expression and explore words and ideas to achieve what I want.

BLUE BIRD BYE-BYE

Our assignment: write a piece that was written as if you are an animal. This rather disturbing (and somewhat humorous) poem was a result. Sorry—but we are what we are on any given day, and on this day I wrote about the cruelty of nature and how we can be surprised by it.

SET

My molestation took place in a basement. When it happened, the acts themselves were just a "thing"—a one-moment-by-moment, slowly-developing "thing." But some "things" go on for eternity— a 60-, 70-, or 80-year eternity. They're permanent. Those acts done against me set my heart toward a path it shouldn't have had to take.

It takes many years and much grace to overcome an act of intentional evil done against an innocent. The images developed in those dark places remain and mar the soul. God comes along and heals, but the scars remain.

GALAXIES

Perhaps my relationship with God is a little different. I see him as a laughing, fun-loving, playful God—almost as often as I see him serious and holy. I observe the way he made the earth and its creatures: long-necked giraffes, fat-butt, big-cheeked hippopotami, anteaters with long snouts and lengthy tongues, and peculiar fish that dangle their own bait! Seriously? He has to have a glorious sense of humor, and he's wildly creative.

So, when I wrote this, I imagined him experiencing colossal joy as he created the heavens and the earth—like a child at play in a sand box—fully delighted over all that his hands and words were creating.

I can envision him roaring in laughter as the galaxies were set in motion. And perhaps, just perhaps—he even did a cartwheel or two.

A PAINTER CAME

Nature's beauty captures me. In this poem, I personified nature and imagined a creative imp climbing trees with a magic paintbrush in hand.

In it, I also acknowledge my fear of creative freedom. Creativity is usually a little messy—even expensive. So sometimes it's humbling to even try—especially when you are fairly certain that what you're creating is going to fall short of the reality OR of your imagination.

MYSTERIES

One of my biggest struggles has been understanding and trusting that God is both loving and sovereign. The two don't seem to go together. It is mystery. It's something I've chosen to accept, but it hasn't been an easy acquiescence. This piece is about the seeming contradiction of love and sovereignty. Waves can be gentle or destructive. LOVE sent Christ to DIE. And the way God rules my life doesn't always meet with my approval or seem "good" to me. Sometimes it's just damnably hard.

Still, there is love and beauty in the mystery of this fallen and sometimes nasty world. If you believe that God is in and over all things, then somehow God (and therefore beauty) is also present in the ugly moments of life.

Chapter VIII
SORROW AND COMFORT

CLICK

My mother's emergency trip to the hospital created the atmosphere for this poem. It flung me into a different state of being. I witnessed pain and longed to see it ameliorated. I humbly gave water to her thirsty lips. She thought I was her mother and kept repeating the phrase, "I love you so much, Mother." Even in her mental stupor, love still flowed.

MELANIE—UPON HER DEATH

I watched in horror as my friend faded quickly from stage four cancer. Discovered late, there was no option for surgery. The family gathered to comfort one another and love her well. I remember how close to God I felt as she approached death. It was as if Christ was on the threshold of an etched glass door—simply waiting to take my friend into glory. I don't like death (it is the LAST enemy to fall), but there is a nearness to God in it—an awareness that he is present and only a breath away from the one who is dying. This is great comfort to me—and should be for all of us who watch believers die.

DEBBIE

My friend Debbie nursed her husband while he slowly faded away with dementia. He was still young at the time. She cared for him imperfectly, but she did it steadfastly. When he passed away, I witnessed this woman of faith continue to move forward in trust.

Knowing my Father as I do, I knew it was his grace and mercy that gave her the courage to press on.

I AM NOT DEAD

Sometimes the only proof that I am alive is pain. Pain is part of life—that sounds trite and ridiculously simple, but it is also true. Why am I surprised when suffering comes? When pain comes with emotional struggles—or pain IS the emotional struggle, it can feel like you are breaking down into dust.

WHEN THE LIGHTS WENT OUT

My husband and I had a series of serious things happen in our lives, and I felt utterly hopeless. A friend spoke into my despair on the phone as I drove away from the hospital toward home. It was a deeply felt hopelessness. I "awefulized"—took to the most horrible extreme of awful—about everything. I was weeping so hard that she told me to pull over. She encouraged as I imagined the worst possible outcome for someone I loved. "God will be present in the future," she said.

That brought me such solace, and it still does. This is a reflection on that season and some of the depth of the knowledge of God that came from it. Christ is the speaker.

God is present in our unknown futures. Hallelujah!

THE PHOENIX

Tornadoes tore through Central Alabama, and over 200 people died. Whole communities were turned to rubble as the multiple large storms wreaked havoc on Birmingham's larger metropolitan area. (At least one was an F-5).

I saw the Church arise to rebuild. For years, they built homes and repaired lives as they worked without pay and travelled at their own expense to help.

The Church swelled with compassion and the overflow of God's love became works of faith and sacrificial giving.

Modern myth says that the Phoenix tears can heal.

MAD LOVE

I wrote this poem after someone's death—I can't remember whether it was after the death of my friend or one of my parents. I think it may have been after my friend's horrible suffering from breast cancer—which ultimately invaded multiple organs and her bones. Her suffering was long and painful, and even though it challenged her faith, she continued to stand most Sundays—bald head and shrunken body—with her hands raised in worship.

The contrast between suffering and heaven's joys often hit me. This is the Christian's great hope: eternal mad love.

Chapter IX
FEAR AND COURAGE

GET BACK IN YOUR HOLE

To become who we're called to be requires courage—a courage that defies the darkness.

The courage to write, or paint, teach the Bible, or begin a new life very different from the one you've always known, requires bravery. Overcoming fear of failure or facing the disapproval of others is huge for me.

I expect criticism from this book. I KNOW it will come. To obey my calling means fighting to overcome the fears and trusting God to help me become who I really am, then doing what I'm meant to do. Those evil voices create terror and scream, "Get back in your hole."

DENIAL

Most of us live with some sort of denial. This reflective piece is a list of some of my go-to denials. Often, I'm unaware that I'm doing it—until I am.

Are you guilty of any of these, or do you have your own personal favorites?

IF I KNEW I WAS BELOVED

God through Jesus Christ has declared our beloved-ness. We have been adopted as sons and daughters and declared righteous. We have immediate, constant access to God the Father—and through his Holy Spirit—we are one with him. The pictures and images of the Church in Scripture remind us it is true. We are the Bride. He lavishes his grace on us. He has given us all we need for life and godliness.

I could go on and on. As I've grown in my awareness of my beloved-ness, I have become bolder. My belovedness is a source of great rejoicing and hope. Knowing this should move us to boldly proclaim it to others, so they can also experience the joy, too.

I am, we are—beloved.

SEA SONG

While sitting on the beach, I watched a stingray frolic in the waves. I thought about the unseen things beneath the surface—some frightening—some beautiful. I contemplated the power and vastness of the sea and the apparent joy the little gray ray had as he surfed the waves.

To ride the rhythm of the sea, to swim in its vast and endless currents and explore its depths, requires fearlessness. There is loss of control, for we don't know where the currents will take us. There is danger because we don't know what's beneath us or what's beyond our sight. But, if we don't enjoy the journey, explore, dive, and see the wonder around us, we will abide in fear, eyes darting as we look for the next predator.

The ocean, like God, is too deep and wide to comprehend; we see in part and know in part. To grow as a person of faith, we must live in the mystery of the unseen power of God and ride the depth and majesty of God – no matter what it brings.

THE POET

My friend read her poem after winning a poetry award. She was brave. Brave to write in her pain. Brave to enter the contest. Brave to put herself in a position to be embarrassed. In this poem I celebrated her courage, and at the same time, longed for my own.

THE HOURGLASS RUNS DRY

Time's passing—and fast! One day we wake up with wrinkled faces and gray hair. One day our children are grown, and all dreams are altered and reshaped to fit our age and stage.

In this poetry assignment, we were to begin with, "The hourglass runs dry." It is, as I'm sure you figured out, about courage and choosing to LIVE—truly live in this life God has graciously given.

A PAINTER CAME

The beauty of nature captures me. In this poem, I personified nature and imagined a creative imp climbing trees with a magic paintbrush in hand.

I also acknowledge my fear of the freedom of extravagant creativity. Creativity is usually a little messy and dangerous. As creatives, we put ourselves in a position to be censured and condemned.

Chapter X
TEARS AND LAUGHTER

LONGINGS

I wrote "Longings," "The Eyes of the Lord," and "Enough, I've Had Enough" over several months. During that time, my prayer was answered, but not like I expected.

"Longings" came first. It is a simple cry for more of God and less of me. I was finding too much contentment in my easy abundant life. It was a contentment that didn't take me into the world. I'm still prone toward leisurely pleasure.

"The Eyes of the Lord" was written as God awakened in me a deep sorrow over my indifference. The conviction took me into the jails to teach and into deeper service among women coming out of prison. I'm always afraid to enter into God's sorrow over the world. I'm afraid I'll get swamped in the pain of it all.

As an answer to my prayer in "Longings," I began to experience deep grief over things in the world and at home. That's when I wrote "Enough, I've Had Enough." Sorrow came in buckets; I was overwhelmed with empathy and sympathy for the pain of others. It was a kind of death. But in that poem I remind myself of the earlier poems and see God's answer. He welcomes me into his funeral bower—but in that place—he never leaves me and I am resurrected into a new unexpected life.

When we long to know Christ and to be like Christ, and ask for it, I'm not sure we know what we pray for.

To know Christ is to know deep joy and incredible sorrow. But he is with us in both—laughing, weeping, AND equipping.

AW SHUCKS!

The piece is simply playful for playfulness's sake, with words in each line rhyming. Sometimes I need to play around with words and get my fill of them.

A BOY CAME DOWN THE WALK (A Parody of A Bird Came Down the Walk by Emily Dickinson)

I wrote this as a poetry challenge to parody a famous poem. I chose, "A Bird Came Down the Walk." They are quite similar. I hope you'll look up the original. It was a fun challenge, and I think I did a good job. Enjoy. Laugh.

CADENCE CALLS (to be read like a Jody Call)

I participated in a poetry exercise where I wrote about the Second Coming of Christ. This one is a little silly and fun. I was thinking of the army of the Lord. That led to the idea of cadence calls—the songs that soldiers chant while running together in training. It only becomes playful if you read it like that, with a lilting, singing voice.

AMBROSIA

While traveling with two friends to and from a poetry event, we laughed until we cried. My cheeks ached. There was no alcohol involved, but we got inebriated with friendship and laughter. For me it was life-giving—like ambrosia which, in mythology, is a food or drink that gave immortality and life to the gods.

THIRSTY

This was another silly poem that I wrote as if I'm a dog who is thirsty. It's self-explanatory. Sometimes it's just good to be a little ridiculous and not take oneself too seriously.

Chapter XI
BUSYNESS AND STILLNESS

WAITING

I can be such a ninny. Anxious. Striving. Intense. What God seeks most from me is union with himself. That doesn't come through busyness. It comes through silence, meditation, stillness, and contemplation.

Reality: We have no strength but him.

This poem was written to music.

KABODING

Kabod is the word for glory in Hebrew. It is pronounced (with a short o), but for my purposes, I pronounce it with a long "o." You can do that sort of thing if you have an artist's license. You can borrow mine to read the poem.

This poem is simply about embracing Christ in the stillness of nature and looking for the glory—the kabod, as you do.

SILENCE – ALL YOU UNHOLY VOICES

Anxious thoughts, sinful thoughts, angry or petulant thoughts can invade my soul. This is me shouting at them—telling them to be silent so I can hear God—who speaks in a gentle, loving voice.

THE MUSIC OF SILENCE

I imagined God, through silence, leading a symphony, with each part of creation singing its own silent song of worship and awe. What would a daisy's song be like? I'm certain a mountain would sing bass. The music would be one glorious, holy melody.

SILENCE

Sometimes, when practicing silence, I fall asleep. Most people will experience some level of somnolence when learning contemplative practices. I certainly do. Just go with it. Your body needs a nap.

Chapter XII
DEATH AND LIFE

DOOR OF DEATH

I wrote this when my grandmother died. She was a woman of faith, and those who witnessed her love and faithfulness grieved her loss. We grieve, but the believer who dies, grieves no more.

BORN ALOFT

A young friend lost her husband, leaving her with four young children and a mountain of debt. I wrote this after watching the mourning family. There's something very holy about worshipful grief.

BREATH OF HEAVEN

We watched, worshiped and prayed as my father died. I measured his breath, and watched as the rhythm slowed until it stopped. We wept. We were close to heaven as the door opened to take him home.

WHEN THE SAINTS GO MARCHING IN

I pictured Jesus' final call to his people—the one when he calls us all home—final resurrection—last trumpet. The parts in quotes are words I imagine being spoken by Jesus.

SAILING

One of my sons is a doctor, and my daughter has cared for the dying. Another son has lost young friends to death. Each reminds me that death is capricious in how it chooses to visit. It can come in an instant, approach slowly over years, or advance with great pain and suffering. I am not afraid of dying, because it means eternity with Christ. I **am** concerned about how God puts me in the boat (death). This is about that fear. Elysium's Sea is a mythical ocean between this life and the next.

I HAVE NO POWER HERE

This is also about the death of my father. My mother's and my father's deaths both reminded me of my helplessness. We have no power to determine outcomes. Trusting in God's plan and our future hope is what we do have.

DEATH'S DYING

No explanation needed.

I FIND I WANDER EASILY

I know myself too well. As much as I love Christ, there has always been an allurement to the world that God has had to carve out of me. My faith often waivers. I trust him to keep me, because I do wander easily.

MAY "JESUS" BE MY SIGH

As I watched my mother slowly lose her memory, my greatest longing became this, "Don't let me forget YOUR NAME, O Lord."

I think that the only way to achieve this is through knowing—truly knowing—Christ through his Word and by his Spirit in an intimate relationship.

But ultimately it will be up to God to sustain me. Like in the earlier poem, I have no power here. I can, however, sow in hope, and trust in the promise that he will help me persevere.

My mother's memory disappeared—but God remembered **her** name.

Chapter XIII
WORSHIP

HELP OUR LIPS

This was written as a song of worship. There is a HUGE gap between what we sometimes see and worship and Who God really is. This is a cry to God for help in our attempt to worship him rightly.

O GREAT AND AWESOME GOD AND KING

Sometimes I get so caught up in worship I can barely contain myself. That I know HIM well enough to praise him brings me great joy. That I have the privilege of worshiping and declaring his glories to the world amazes me. I know God—but not like I will one day know him.

COMMUNION SONG

I wrote this song after meditating on the crucifixion.

I OWE SO MUCH

I am utterly dependent on God's grace and mercy. When I consider God's plan of salvation, I am undone. His lavish grace humbles me. Knowing Christ and being intimate with him is a gift of God and something only he can do. I can choose to abide in him and his Word and walk in obedience, but the grace to do this is still from him. It's a mystery.

What is my part? What is his? I don't know. I know I am to cooperate with the Spirit as he leads, prompts, convicts, and helps me remember. He is good when things don't appear "good" and cooperation with him means I am choosing the best, highest road.

FOR CHRIST ALONE

During a study of Ephesians, I wrote this. If you want to be fully awed, read Ephesians over and over again. Meditate on each verse. God's gifts to his people are breathtakingly glorious.

ACKNOWLEDGMENTS

Many urged me to compile my poems. You saved them and told me of their impact. Thank you for loving my babies; it fueled my courage.

Special folks are my cheerleaders. First, I must mention Nancy Carroll. Your faithful nudges over twenty years keep me moving toward becoming who I am—beloved and creative. Sue Tolle, you've steadily cheered and supported me. Thank you, Nancy, Marjean Brooks, Michele Bullock, and Charlotte Donlon. Your insight during writer's group forces me to edit my work more carefully. Thank you, Anne Riley, for helping edit.

Three friends quickly offered financial support when I told them about the project. Thank you. Your three-fold, anonymous support confirmed the call and gave me the resolve to continue moving forward. I recall your offers when I get discouraged. Britta Lafont and Lisa Donohue, you knew the ins and outs of Create Space and dared me to believe that with your help, I could do this. You have loved and encouraged me this year. A new friend, Frances Higginbotham, designed the cover. I didn't see your kindness coming. Meg Flowers gave me a two-inch carved rooster from Israel because she recalled the poem, "Peter's Song." You didn't know about the project, but you gave it at a time when I doubted the merit of my labor.

I must also thank my dear husband, Raymond, for giving me space to write. Without your faithful love and tenderness, I'm not sure who I would be today. My friends and family provided much of the fodder for my poetry. I love you and watch your lives. Your faith, pain, and tenacity has guided my pen and spoken to my soul.

My pastor, Bob Flayhart, your unmitigated courage to preach grace and truth weekly has powered my faith and spiritual growth. Thank you.

Finally, I must, give a standing ovation to Noel Fagan. You edited my work and did it with tenderness, love, and a poet's heart. I read your comments and suggestions with worship, tears, and amazement. I wish I could insert your comments. Your responses are what I hope others will experience as they read these chapters. I can't wait for your poems to be printed one day.

I also praise, thank, and worship my Trinitarian God who has nurtured my soul, and is still in the process of delivering my mad, self-loathing, sinful, busy, doubting, sorrowful, fearful, impure, and wrestling heart. You, in your grace and love, still amaze me and bring me to tears.

ABOUT THE POET

Linda Barrett is the wife of one kind-hearted man and mother to three adult children. She teaches, mentors, plays, and writes in Birmingham, Alabama. She has a doctor's degree in life and a B.A. in English. She has published several devotional articles and co-authored a young mother's devotional book, *Engaging Motherhood: Heart Preparation for a Holy Calling.*

She blogs unfaithfully at aninvitationtowonder.wordpress.com.

Her email address is lindarcb31@yahoo.com.

REFERENCES

English Standard Version (ESV)

The Holy Bible, English Standard Version. ESV® Text Edition: 2016. Copyright © 2001 by Crossway Bibles, a publishing ministry of Good News Publishers.

New American Standard Bible (NASB)

Copyright © 1960, 1962, 1963, 1968, 1971, 1972, 1973, 1975, 1977, 1995 by The Lockman Foundation NIV

New Century Version (NCV)

The Holy Bible, New Century Version®. Copyright © 2005 by Thomas Nelson, Inc.

New English Translation (NET)

NET Bible® copyright ©1996-2006 by Biblical Studies Press, L.L.C. http://netbible.com All rights reserved.

New International Version (NIV)

Holy Bible, New International Version®, NIV® Copyright ©1973, 1978, 1984, 2011 by Biblica, Inc.® Used by permission. All rights reserved worldwide.

Manning, Brennan; (2003) The Rabbi's Heartbeat; Colorado Springs, CO NavPressPublishingGroup

The Chronicles of Narnia: the Lion the Witch and The Wardrobe Walt Disney - 2006

Made in the USA
Lexington, KY
05 December 2018